Empowered by Wisdom

Empowered by Wisdom

By

Dr. Freddy B. Wilson

Empowered By Wisdom
Copyright © 2017 by Dr. Freddy B. Wilson. All rights reserved.
No part of this publication may be reproduced, stored in a retrieval system or transmitted in any way by any means, electronic, mechanical, photocopy, recording or otherwise without the prior permission of the author except as provided by USA copyright law.
The opinions expressed by the author are not necessarily those of Wilsonet Enterprises
Published by Wilsonet Enterprises
135 Bonnie Lane | Fayetteville, Georgia 30215 USA
404-754-0858 |
Wilsonet Enterprises is committed to excellence.
Book design copyright © 2017 by Wilsonet Enterprises. All rights reserved.
Cover design by Dr. Freddy B. Wilson
Published in the United States of America
ISBN: 978-0-9987873-0-5
1. Religion / Christian Life / Personal Growth
2. Family And Relationship/General
14.10.28

Empowered By Wisdom

Introduction

Wisdom is not always understood for what it really is. Some people get wisdom confused with knowledge. Having knowledge does not necessarily mean you have wisdom. Knowledge is simply the tacit information one can gather or obtain about certain matters, situations, circumstances, or events. Wisdom is the ability to use this information and applying it to work successfully through and beyond the matter at hand. Wisdom can be used in a worldly sense but only godly wisdom will withstand the test of time. There are many examples of wisdom being applied in the bible.

The story of Esther in the bible exemplifies having wisdom. Esther was shown to be faithful, patriotic, and courageous. She was dedicated to the needs of her father and anxious to share the king's favor with him. As a good wife to the king, she used her wisdom to influence him favorably for many years. Her wisdom enabled her to obtain favor from all she came in contact with.

Esther 2:15 (NLT) [15]Esther was the daughter of Abihail, who was Mordecai's uncle. (Mordecai had adopted his younger cousin Esther.) When it was Esther's turn to go to the king, she accepted the advice of Hegai, the eunuch in charge of the harem. She asked for nothing except what he suggested, and

Empowered By Wisdom

> she was admired by everyone who saw her.

Esther was wise enough not to abuse her favor with the king but generous enough to take care of others. Her selflessness was a sure sign of having wisdom to know she needed to make a difference in the lives of others. As Esther realized, wisdom is waiting for you to realize you need to reach out and take a hold on wisdom to better your life. You have to have enough wisdom to know God is in control and you are not. No matter how much you achieve in education, business, or your career, you can't outdo what God can do for you and you should give God the credit for all you were able to achieve.

> **Proverbs 8:1-5 (NLT)** [1] Listen as Wisdom calls out! Hear as understanding raises her voice! [2] On the hilltop along the road, she takes her stand at the crossroads. [3] By the gates at the entrance to the town, on the road leading in, she cries aloud, [4] "I call to you, to all of you! I raise my voice to all people. [5] You simple people, use good judgment. You foolish people, show some understanding.

True wisdom does not come easily. You have to be wise enough to withstand correction from others or directly from

Empowered By Wisdom

God, no matter how successful, accomplished, or educated you are. Some people think of themselves as being so prominent in their individual jobs, positions, or specialties that they will only listen to certain people. These certain people they listen to normally held positions considered higher or more prestigious. Allow me to give you a word of advice - listen to what others are saying to you! God will bless you with discernment to know what information is good and what information is not. You never know through whom God is sending you a message. Be willing to accept good advice.

> **Proverbs 13:13-15 (NLT)** [13] People who despise advice are asking for trouble; those who respect a command will succeed. [14] The instruction of the wise is like a life-giving fountain; those who accept it avoid the snares of death. [15] A person with good sense is respected; a treacherous person is headed for destruction.

Never get so big that you cannot listen to others. No person knows everything and you are not so important that you are the only wise person around. Having a lot of knowledge does not make you wise. Proverbs 21:11 says if you punish a mocker, the simpleminded become wise; if you instruct the wise, they will be all the wiser.

Empowered By Wisdom

Knowledge vs. Wisdom

There is a difference between knowledge and wisdom. Noted philosopher Arthur Schopenhauer formulated a foundation that all knowledge was derived from our experience of the world but that our experience was necessarily subjective and formed by our own intellect and biases. Therefore, reality is simply an extension of our own will. (Schopenhauer, 2004)

> **1 Corinthians 8:1-3 (NLT)** [1]Now regarding your question about food that has been offered to idols. Yes, we know that "we all have knowledge" about this issue. But while knowledge makes us feel important, it is love that strengthens the church. [2]Anyone who claims to know all the answers doesn't really know very much. [3]But the person who loves God is the one whom God recognizes.

This passage shows that everyone has access to knowledge. As a part of our education, we gain a lot of knowledge over the years. Many times the knowledge gained was beneficial. However, some of us will use that knowledge to make it appear that we are better than other people. We have become impressed with knowledge and even sometimes consider what we have is wisdom.

Empowered By Wisdom

> **Proverbs 3:7-10 (NLT)** ⁷ Don't be impressed with your own wisdom. Instead, fear the LORD and turn away from evil. ⁸ Then you will have healing for your body and strength for your bones. ⁹ Honor the LORD with your wealth and with the best part of everything you produce. ¹⁰ Then he will fill your barns with grain, and your vats will overflow with good wine.

There are many circumstances where our knowledge won't be enough to become the wisdom that will enable us the get out of our circumstances. Psalms 111:10 says the fear of the Lord is the beginning of wisdom. We must always acknowledge God in all we do and ask him for the wisdom and courage we need to use our faith to move forward in our lives. Yes, it takes wisdom and courage for us to exercise our faith. Wisdom will give us what we need to do something and courage will give us the boost to act on that information. It takes a lot to act on our faith, especially when people around you don't believe you're capable of tackling the challenge you're facing.

> **Proverbs 3:13-20 (NLT)** ¹³ Joyful is the person who finds wisdom, the one who gains understanding. ¹⁴ For wisdom is more profitable than silver, and her wages are better than gold. ¹⁵ Wisdom is more precious than rubies; nothing you desire can compare with her. ¹⁶ She offers

> you long life in her right hand, and riches and honor in her left. [17] She will guide you down delightful paths; all her ways are satisfying. [18] Wisdom is a tree of life to those who embrace her; happy are those who hold her tightly. [19] By wisdom the LORD founded the earth; by understanding he created the heavens. [20] By his knowledge the deep fountains of the earth burst forth, and the dew settles beneath the night sky.

Early twentieth century Scottish Christian minister and teacher, Oswald Chambers, said, "The way we continually talk about our own inabilities is an insult to our Creator. To complain over our incompetence is to accuse God falsely of having overlooked us. Get into the habit of examining from God's perspective those things that sound so humble to men. You will be amazed at how unbelievably inappropriate and disrespectful they are to Him. We say things such as, 'Oh, I shouldn't claim to be sanctified; I'm not a saint.' But to say that before God means, 'No, Lord, it is impossible for You to save and sanctify me; there are opportunities I have not had and so many imperfections in my brain and body; no, Lord, it isn't possible.' That may sound wonderfully humble to others, but before God it is an attitude of defiance." (Chambers, 2012)

Chambers said that conversely, "the things that sound humble before God may sound exactly the opposite to people. To say, 'Thank God, I know I am saved and sanctified,' is in God's eyes the purest expression of humility. It means you have so completely surrendered yourself to God that you know He is true. Never worry about whether what you say sounds humble before others or not. But always be humble before God, and allow Him to be your all in all.

There is only one relationship that really matters, and that is your personal relationship to your personal Redeemer and Lord. If you maintain that at all costs, letting everything else go, God will fulfill His purpose through your life. One individual life may be of priceless value to God's purposes, and yours may be that life."

Godly Wisdom Over Worldly Wisdom

You never know what God is up to. That is why it is much more important to possess Godly wisdom than worldly wisdom. Godly wisdom comes only when you seek God's guidance in your daily walk and your daily decisions. You should focus your steps on what will please God and all other things will fall into place.

Colossians 3:2 says you should think about the things of heaven, not the things of earth. For you died to this life, and your real life is hidden with Christ in God. When you use this kind of wisdom, peace and tranquility will follow. Doing what God will have you do always ends up to your benefit. You will find all your answers to your questions in Christ, our Lord.

> **Colossians 3:15-17 (NLT)** [15]And let the peace that comes from Christ rule in your hearts. For as members of one body you are called to live in peace. And always be thankful. [16]Let the message about Christ, in all its richness, fill your lives. Teach and counsel each other with all the wisdom he gives. Sing psalms and hymns and spiritual songs to God with thankful hearts. [17]And whatever you do or say, do it as a representative of the Lord Jesus, giving thanks through him to God the Father.

Empowered By Wisdom

When you go to work you should do as I do - ask the Lord to bless you to complete the things that please him. Always ask for his grace in your workday. Even when you go through problems at work it has its purpose. Your attitude and approach to problems may be God's way of showing others how his people respond to problems in faith verses working, "the system". I can witness to the power of surrendering your all to God when dealing with work situations. One of my latest work situations had me feeling really bad because I wasn't promoted to leading my unit after my former boss departed. Upper management sent someone else to be in charge. I was really upset at this and the change with the new boss was initially traumatic. After I had to finally realize that all that I went through and whatever my new boss had to go through when moving to my location, it all had a purpose. I got strength when I told the Lord my life is in His hands and I fully trust only Him. My life at work got better and I then became fully confident in God that a special blessing was coming. I stopped worrying about my situation and told the Lord I will stay faithful and continue to work diligently towards pleasing Him and not worrying about people on the job. And yes, that blessing did come less than a year later. I now know that God is not finished with me after I received the blessing I received when I placed my trust solely in God's hands. People may hurt you and even hinder you from progressing to where you want to go; however, they can't stop what God wants for you.

Colossians 3:23-25 (NLT) [23]Work willingly at whatever you do, as though you were working for the Lord rather

> than for people. ²⁴Remember that the Lord will give you an inheritance as your reward, and that the Master you are serving is Christ. ²⁵But if you do what is wrong, you will be paid back for the wrong you have done. For God has no favorites.

God placed humans on earth to have dominion over the plants and animals. This does not mean that we can just do what we want. Pastor Rodney Akins of Restoration Family Life Center (RFLC), Jonesboro, GA said we need to move in a direction that pleases God. We are in the image of God so we need act more like we belong to God and we don't just "exist". Pastor Akins provided the following attributes of God:

- Unique, 1 Peter 2:9 said we are peculiar people:

> **1 Peter 2:9 (NLT)** But you are not like that, for you are a chosen people. You are royal priests, a holy nation, God's very own possession. As a result, you can show others the goodness of God, for he called you out of the darkness into his wonderful light.

- God Is Love (1 John 4:8). We need to follow his will. We can't fail if we seek God's will in our lives.

- God is a theistic God, not a deistic God. Rational Wiki said, "The difference rests on the difference between a theistic god that is interested in, if not actively involved in, the outcome of his creation and humanity specifically and a deistic god that is either disinterested in the outcome, and holds no special place for humanity, or will not intervene." God is theistic in that he is concerned with each of our personal matters. We can and should have a personal relationship with him.

> **Matthew 6:26 (NLT)** Look at the birds. They don't plant or harvest or store food in barns, for your heavenly Father feeds them. And aren't you far more valuable to him than they are?

- God is consistent. He has never changed, nor will He!

> **Hebrews 13:8 (NLT)** Jesus Christ is the same yesterday, today, and forever.

There are many things of the world we can seek. Many of them are useless if we don't make God a part of what we have and what we do. I have previously written about dealing with the facts in our lives by recognizing the truth of God's greatness. You have to understand that you have to go through something in order for God to get you to another place in your life. We can acknowledge the facts, but state God's truth to our situations. God is in front providing for you while protecting you from the back. You must believe that your purpose and progress is a process. An example of this is in Exodus when Pharaoh changed his mind about freeing the Israelites and started to pursue them.

> **Exodus 14:5 - 7 (NLT)** [5]When word reached the king of Egypt that the Israelites had fled, Pharaoh and his officials changed their minds. "What have we done, letting all those Israelite slaves get away?" they asked. [6]So Pharaoh harnessed his chariot and called up his troops. [7]He took with him 600 of Egypt's best chariots, along with the rest of the chariots of Egypt, each with its commander.

> **Exodus 14:14 (NLT)** [14]The LORD himself will fight for you. Just stay calm."

> **Exodus 14:19 (NLT)** [19]Then the angel of God, who had been leading the people of Israel, moved to the rear of the camp. The pillar of cloud also moved from the front and stood behind them.

Exodus 14:26 - 28 (NLT) ²⁶When all the Israelites had reached the other side, the LORD said to Moses, "Raise your hand over the sea again. Then the waters will rush back and cover the Egyptians and their chariots and charioteers." ²⁷So as the sun began to rise, Moses raised his hand over the sea, and the water rushed back into its usual place. The Egyptians tried to escape, but the LORD swept them into the sea. ²⁸Then the waters returned and covered all the chariots and charioteers—the entire army of Pharaoh. Of all the Egyptians who had chased the Israelites into the sea, not a single one survived.

Empowered By Wisdom

Wisdom Provides Power to Deal with Family Life

The Bible speaks of wisdom in dealing with family life in the book of Peter.

> **1 Peter 3:7 (NLT)** [7]In the same way, you husbands must give honor to your wives. Treat your wife with understanding as you live together. She may be weaker than you are, but she is your equal partner in God's gift of new life. Treat her as you should so your prayers will not be hindered.

There is an order to the family that must be adhered to. In the book, "No Other Way, Establishing God's Standard For The Family" by Dr. LaSalle R. Vaughn, Dr. Myles Munroe was quoted as saying, "The key to healing the community and society, and thus the nation, is healing, restoring, and strengthening the family." (Vaughn, 1993) Your family should be the most important thing to you next to your relationship with God.

Dr. Vaughn said, "Our answer is to follow God's plan. Only His plan for the family will work. Only by following God's plan will our marriages, our families, be able to withstand all the attacks of the devil." When we hear such words, we must have the wisdom to know how to apply this information to our lives.

Vaughn said, "We must stand for family values, because family values are God's values. The family is important to God. God established the family, and His Church is a family, and the Bible tells us that marriages are supposed to be patterned on the relationship of Christ and His Church."

In our book, "The Power of Christian Friendship", my co-author and I spoke of the importance of friendship in a relationship, particularly in marriage. (Wilson & Armster, 2010) Vaughn said that we will have to look at the values we live by, not just in marriage, but in dating and in preparing for marriage. Vaughn said, "We need to prepare for marriage according to God's plan, and choose our mates according to His plan. Problems in marriage affect the family. You can't get away from it. When a husband and a wife are not on one accord, it's going to affect the children. And most of those problems come from people being selfish in their marriages." Even if a husband and wife disagree on an issue, they must operate in one accord.

That is my idea of having wisdom. This sort of wisdom will bring about the unity we need in families. I agree with Vaughn when he said that dinner is a good time for family fellowship, even though sometimes the spouses and even the children are so busy, they want to go do their own thing. Absence of unity causes confusion within a family. The kids end up not knowing what to expect and or not trusting parents.

If you don't have family meetings, now is a good time to start. Some of your family members may not like the idea and give you push back. You will have to stand your ground and create order in your family. Vaughn said, "You have to have order. A man is the pastor of his home. Some of us think we're called to be pastors of churches. First, we have to pastor the sheep God has given us; our wives and our children. That's your congregation. Your wife is your co-pastor. Your children are your members." Additionally, Vaughn said, "A lot of families don't care enough to establish goals, or to work together to meet the family or individual goals. The husband and wives only care about themselves, about being happy. There's more at stake. There's more to life than your happiness."

We must have enough wisdom to know that our personal satisfaction does not have to be fulfilled, especially if it is a detriment to our family. Vaughn said that this focus on individual happiness has contributed to the loss of respect for men in the United States. "Many women are disappointed in men, because society leads them to expect so much. And it kills the men on the inside, particularly black men. We need women to help us to be men. We're asking you to let us be men. There's nothing worse than a manipulated man. There's nothing worse than a woman who can manipulate a man to get him to do anything she wants. When a woman manipulates a man so much that he can't think for himself, he will never reach the full potential God has planned for him. He will never be the man that God has called him to be." There are some wives that try to manipulate their husbands to the point the husband feels too constrained to do anything out of fear the wives won't like what they are doing. This could lead to frustration.

Empowered By Wisdom

Men should take the lead in their families, but this does not mean that women should be seen as a lesser being. 1 Corinthians 16:13-14 says to be on guard. Stand firm in the faith. Be courageous. Be strong. And do everything with love. Vaughn said that men must be careful never to dominate women, "to dominate a woman to the point where she can't be her own person and celebrate her uniqueness is a definite turn off to her. God never intended men to dominate women. Domination can be a form of control and manipulation. Domination, control and manipulation will hinder your wife from becoming the person God intended her to be. There needs to be a balance there. That means putting our family values ahead of our own desires and our own egos. Otherwise we're bringing trouble to our families. Proverbs 11:29 says he who brings trouble on his family will inherit only wind, and the fool will be servant to the wise."

We must learn to love our families in God's way. I have learned that the most excellent quality of life is love. The best way to teach another person love is to show them love. You should ask yourself, are you loving on the right level? In a relationship, you sometimes will have to take the high road to problems and take the blame when it's not your fault. You should know that undeserved generosity and patience will show unconditional commitment and undeserved friendship. Please teach your family how to forgive and give respect for those in authority. Wisdom will show you how to have cheerful generosity and to show love in correction.

Empowered By Wisdom

> **Matthew 5:43-48 (NLT)** [43]"You have heard the law that says, 'Love your neighbor and hate your enemy. [44]But I say, love your enemies! Pray for those who persecute you! [45]In that way, you will be acting as true children of your Father in heaven. For he gives his sunlight to both the evil and the good, and he sends rain on the just and the unjust alike. [46]If you love only those who love you, what reward is there for that? Even corrupt tax collectors do that much. [47]If you are kind only to your friends, how are you different from anyone else? Even pagans do that. [48]But you are to be perfect, even as your Father in heaven is perfect.

Sometimes God will bless you with a conditional blessing. This means you were blessed not because you did something great or worked to deserve the blessing. He blesses you simply because you were witting to follow his rules and obedient to His directions. The opposite of this are those that are cursed because of their resistance and rebellion.

> **Psalms 37:23-37 (NLT)** [23] The LORD directs the steps of the godly. He delights in every detail of their lives. [24] Though they stumble, they will never fall, for the LORD holds them by the

Empowered By Wisdom

hand. 25 Once I was young, and now I am old. Yet I have never seen the godly abandoned or their children begging for bread. 26 The godly always give generous loans to others, and their children are a blessing. 27 Turn from evil and do good, and you will live in the land forever. 28 For the LORD loves justice, and he will never abandon the godly. He will keep them safe forever, but the children of the wicked will die. 29 The godly will possess the land and will live there forever. 30 The godly offer good counsel; they teach right from wrong. 31 They have made God's law their own, so they will never slip from his path. 32 The wicked wait in ambush for the godly, looking for an excuse to kill them. 33 But the LORD will not let the wicked succeed or let the godly be condemned when they are put on trial. 34 Put your hope in the LORD. Travel steadily along his path. He will honor you by giving you the land. You will see the wicked destroyed. 35 I have seen wicked and ruthless people flourishing like a tree in its native soil. 36 But when I looked again, they were gone! Though I searched for them, I could not find them! 37 Look at those who are honest and good, for a wonderful future awaits those who love peace.

Empowered By Wisdom

If you want to progress, you must believe God for new possibilities in life. There are seven tips I've learned that can help you:

1. Avoid the generation of complainers. They will discourage you.

2. Disconnect from those that carry dissention. They will confuse you.

3. Seek new ways to look at offences. They are there to make you stronger.

4. Respond differently about irritation. Your response will determine its outcome.

5. Learn how to see problems leaving you. Each problem is temporary.

6. Don't wait until crisis to call God. I learned before you do anything, pray first!

7. Keep focus on God's blessings. His possibilities are endless.

When you get the wisdom that only God can provide, he will bless you with extraordinary ideas that you can apply to life and your circumstances. This wisdom can be applied so you can learn to gain and keep special people in your life. This is important so you can have positive influences around you. On the other hand, wisdom can teach you how to deal with the devil. You must learn how to recognize attacks from the devil. Always continue to praise God during the devil's attacks.

Wisdom Provides the Power to Deal with Relationships

I have come to learn that one of the greatest battles for single men or women is the flesh, whether it is sex, whether it is loneliness, whether it is just intense personal battles. I agree with Vaughn that, "Single women and men need to make a commitment to wholeness before they enter into a relationship and especially marriage."

"Commitments in marriage can distract a person from his or her commitment to God. For some, it is better not to get their lives so involved. Look at Corinthians 7:7-9. For some people, it's better to stay single." Paul said:

> **1 Corinthians 7:7-9 (NLT)** 7But I wish everyone were single, just as I am. But God gives to some the gift of marriage, and to others the gift of singleness. 8So I say to those who aren't married and to widows—it's better to stay unmarried, just as I am. 9But if they can't control themselves, they should go ahead and marry. It's better to marry than to burn with lust.

Too many men and women are more concerned about pleasing their mates than pleasing God. Instead of serving God more, they focus on keeping the peace in their homes. Vaughn said, "God loved us while we were still sinners. Love means accepting someone for who he or she is. Don't ever fall in love with someone solely on his or her potential. They may never reach their potential."

You should always seek growth in your life. This includes your walk with Christ and in your relationship with your mate! Vaughn said, "We know that we serve a holy God. And sin separates us, not just from God, but from each other. Jesus Christ unites us. He makes it possible to unite with our holy God and with each other, to grow closer to God and to each other. This is what we should be looking forward to when we get married: growth. And growth only comes when you allow the truth to free you." There is an old adage that when a person shows you who they are, believe them the first time! Don't get so lost in your feeling for or emotions over a person that you don't pay attention to their problem areas you don't like.

2 Timothy 2:22 said to run from anything that stimulates youthful lusts. Instead, pursue righteous living, faithfulness, love, and peace. Enjoy the companionship of those who call on the Lord with pure hearts. Vaughn said, "Your relationship must be one of caring – deep, close friendship. There are different levels of friendship. Friendship can enter intimacy – deep close friendships with persons of the opposite sex. If you're getting intimate, does the other person really care for you? People who get into affairs

mostly enter friendships, and then they go deeper and deeper."

The other side of this is infatuation. Infatuation gives you an immature relationship that brings you pain, crying, and hurt most of the time. These immature relationships take away your self-image. Vaughn said, "Mature relationships energize you, make you feel good about yourself. You get up in the morning and sing. Life is just great." Infatuation can be in a form of lust for the other person's appearance. There is nothing wrong with being attracted to a person physically; however, if that's the only redeeming quality for that person you're in for a rude awakening!

I agree with Vaughn when he said, "Real love is conceived when two people enter emotional intimacy – not dependency. Emotional intimacy is a strong feeling, a desire, a longing to be with the other person. This emotional intimacy should be the foundation of the relationship. It should not be sexual. You can be intimate without being sexual. To be intimate means to reveal yourself to each other, learning to listen and give of yourself to each other. It should be a mutual thing. But there are times when just one person allows himself or herself to enter emotional intimacy with another person, and the other person is not there. That's when you say one person's in love and other person's not."

Vaughn also said, "One of the greatest needs a woman has in a marriage is to know that she's loved. Once she knows that she's loved for who she is, and appreciated, you don't have to have any money. You don't have to have a bunch of things."

"The next one is security – not just to be secure in the physical sense, but to be secure in her husband's love, to know you're not going to run out on her after she has two or three children for you. Women want to be valued for who they are. Respect is another major need. So are fidelity, honesty, trust and affection – women like to be touched. Love demands touching."

As I was writing this portion of this book I experienced unforeseen problems dealing with my family living apart. Sometimes we ask the Lord why we are dealing with a certain problem but we aren't prepared for the answer. If your living by God's will everything you experience has its purpose. We must learn to use wisdom to dominate our situations.

There are ways we can dominate our situations. I've learned in the past to not let others or situations dominate your joy. God put in us a spirit of excellence. Even though you are facing a problem, use the wisdom God gives you to speak over things that will come to past. You don't have to be so negative about the negative things you face. You have to speak health and wealth into your life.

You must use your God-given image to create your world. God put in man a spirit of growth that enables him to expand and increase. In the physical world, our health is determined by what we eat. This also applies to spiritual health. You have to continually feed your spirit. The choices we make has a big influence on our lives.

> **Psalms 1:1-3 (NLT)** ¹ Oh, the joys of those who do not follow the advice of the wicked, or stand around with sinners, or join in with mockers. ² But they delight in the law of the LORD, meditating on it day and night. ³ They are like trees planted along the riverbank, bearing fruit each season. Their leaves never wither, and they prosper in all they do.

God has an answer to every problem in His Word. When you have a problem in your family, pray first, then look to the bible for answers. Don't let your family become unhealthy by feeding them junk or letting them starve, both physically and spiritually. The parable of the barren fig tree is a good example of what a family needs:

> **Luke 13:6 - 9 (NLT)** ⁶Then Jesus told this story: "A man planted a fig tree in his garden and came again and again to see if there was any fruit on it, but he was always disappointed. ⁷Finally, he said to his gardener, 'I've waited three years, and there hasn't been a single fig! Cut it down. It's just taking up space in the garden.' ⁸"The gardener answered, 'Sir, give it one more chance. Leave it another year, and I'll give it special attention and plenty of fertilizer. ⁹If we get figs next year, fine. If not, then you can cut it down.'"

Don't be like the garden owner by planting a tree and not tend to it. God blessed you with a family and you need to do what it takes for it to grow and become fruitful. You must attend to your family and provide unconditional love (fertilizer).

There are three areas you can grow your family:

1. Spiritual – remember everything big is not blessed. This can include big houses, big and expensive cars, and large bank accounts. You must keep your eye on God and not what's in His hands. 2 Peter 3:18 (NLT) says, "...you must grow in the grace and knowledge of our Lord and Savior Jesus Christ. All glory to him, both now and forever! Amen".

2. Love – As the old adage goes, love can overcome a multitude of sins. I think this includes a multitude of offenses as well. Remain hopeful for your love ones.

> **1 Thessalonians 1:3 (NLT)** ³As we pray to our God and Father about you, we think of your faithful work, your loving deeds, and the enduring hope you have because of our Lord Jesus Christ.

3. Vision – every generation should have increased vision. A lot of vision comes from exposure. You

should expose your family to good things in life. Maybe the next generation can yearn for something better in life. You should let them know all things are possible through Christ.

> **Ephesians 5:15 - 17 (NLT)** [15]So be careful how you live. Don't live like fools, but like those who are wise. [16]Make the most of every opportunity in these evil days. [17]Don't act thoughtlessly, but understand what the Lord wants you to do.

You must work towards a healthy relationship within the family. Sometimes this may mean departing from the ways you were raised. Many of us think our past lives living at home as children was just so wonderful. Some of us may not see the dysfunction that was within our families and we try to raise and treat our children the same way we were treated. Some of our past families lives went beyond dysfunction but is not considered abuse. Either way you look at your past life, there must be order in the family.

Some of us have unknown low self-esteem based on what we were told or how we felt about ourselves as children. I'm not trying to be a psychologist but some of the problems you're dealing with now are based on your own dysfunctional actions you committed based on how you see yourself and how you try to manage your personal outlook on life. I must ask, "Do you love yourself?" I have always felt and observed that you can't fully love someone else if you don't love yourself. In order for you to show full love for your family, you must first learn to love yourself.

Some people think it's showing love by buying things for their love ones or their kids. I'm not bashing anyone for having things or money (I will discuss this more later). I'm just saying that STUFF doesn't produce order in your family. Sometimes it can just create confusion in the meaning of love. If you're going to buy something for your family members, do so in good taste and do not try to use it to control or influence them.

Your life with your family should be orderly, arranged, and systematic. You, as a believer, man or woman, must be willing to set the example for your family. You must look to Christ, and make the steps He directs you to take.

> **Psalms 119:1-3 (NLT)** [1] Joyful are people of integrity, who follow the instructions of the LORD. [2] Joyful are those who obey his laws and search for him with all their hearts. [3] They do not compromise with evil, and they walk only in his paths.

> **Psalms 37:23-24 (NLT)** [23] The LORD directs the steps of the godly. He delights in every detail of their lives. [24] Though they stumble, they will never

fall, for the LORD holds them by the hand.

I learned some time ago that God does not operate in confusion. To keep confusion down, you must first establish order in the family. Everyone must be in his or her place. Before that can happen you must, as Christ taught, know your place.

> **1 Corinthians 11:3 (NLT)** ³But there is one thing I want you to know: The head of every man is Christ, the head of woman is man, and the head of Christ is God.

Once we get in our proper places, we must start resetting priorities. This means that God comes first, your family second, and the vision you set for your family comes next. It's good to be generous to strangers, neighbors, and others but you must provide for your own family first.

> **1 Timothy 5:8 (NLT)** ⁸But those who won't care for their relatives, especially those in their own household, have denied the true faith. Such people are worse than unbelievers.

Somewhere in the bible it states where there is no vision, the people perish. I think this is true for without some sort of vision your family don't know where they are going or what to expect out of life. Living publicly as a Christian will subject you to a lot of criticism. When your spouse or children speak to unbelievers about things your family expect God to bless you with, they will think you are crazy. We must not concern ourselves with what others think about us during our walk of faith with Christ.

> ***Proverbs 29:25-26 (NLT)*** *25 Fearing people is a dangerous trap, but trusting the LORD means safety. 26 Many seek the ruler's favor, but justice comes from the LORD.*

In order to move forward in our lives under a clear vision, we must learn to alter everyday practices. One of my former pastors taught me that uncommon men do daily what common men do occasionally. We must move intentionally on matters in our daily lives with a purpose. There's got to be a "must" in your daily life. We pray regularly for God to guide us in His will. If you give God what He wants and He'll give you what you want.

All this will support your having a blessed family. Unfortunately, many societies are defining being blessed mainly on material things a person or a family owns. I have learned that blessings are not indicated by the stuff you own. There is nothing wrong with having stuff or possessions so long as you give God the praise for your things and not worship or honor the things you own.

> **Psalms 112:1-3 (NLT)** ¹ Praise the LORD! How joyful are those who fear the LORD and delight in obeying his commands. ² Their children will be successful everywhere; an entire generation of godly people will be blessed. ³ They themselves will be wealthy, and their good deeds will last forever.

I know many of you have heard people who talk about the evil of money. You can bet that the people who are saying such things are not rich. You don't have to be rich to be blessed and God does not ordain poverty. God never meant for any of us to be poor. Contrary to many portrayals and beliefs, Jesus was not always poor. Jesus became poor to help us understand God's greatness.

> **2 Corinthians 8:9 (NLT)** ⁹You know the generous grace of our Lord Jesus Christ. Though he was rich, yet for your sakes he became poor, so that by his poverty he could make you rich.

You must learn to speak greatness into existence in your life. Stop telling yourself that you'll always be poor or will never have enough. Say to yourself, "God wants me to be rich". Understand and believe that Jesus became what I was (poor) so I can become what He was (rich). Say to yourself, "Wealth and riches shall be in my house". Don't be envious of other people's status or what they have. Remember that God blesses good and bad people. God blesses in spite of you. God is not poor and He does not want you to be poor.

> **2 John 1:2-3 (NLT)** ²because the truth lives in us and will be with us forever. ³Grace, mercy, and peace, which come from God the Father and from Jesus Christ—the Son of the Father—will continue to be with us who live in truth and love.

While we're on the subject of money there are two major factors that happen in families related to money. I guess you can call this portion, "love and money".

1. Lack of finances or a lack of money is a family stressor. Let's face it, you do need money to survive and take care of your family. Having money is only a problem if it controls you or you use it to control others. If you don't have a lot of money, you should be at least thankful for what you have. Then you should be faithful that God will provide for you. If you're faithful over a little, God makes you a

master of a lot. I have seen and experienced when God can bless you to do a lot without a lot of money.

2. Money and wealth without spiritual maturity is a problem. Believe it or not, you can have money and still not have joy. Don't ever assume that all rich people are happy. With money comes a host of other things and problems to deal with. Money can't save you from everything.

> **1 Timothy 6:9-10 (NLT)** ⁹But people who long to be rich fall into temptation and are trapped by many foolish and harmful desires that plunge them into ruin and destruction. ¹⁰For the love of money is the root of all kinds of evil. And some people, craving money, have wandered from the true faith and pierced themselves with many sorrows.

Your family needs your love, understanding, and compassion more than they need your money. You must get your family in order so when money does come, it will not ruin your relationships or your family life. There are three things you must do to prepare for wealth:

1. Move from fear to faith. Too many times in life you've tried to make things work and you couldn't make it work. Failure makes you afraid to try again or believe that things could change to being

positive. You have to shake off the weight of failure and turn to God and never doubt him.

> **Matthew 14:27-31 (NLT)** ²⁷But Jesus spoke to them at once. "Don't be afraid," he said. "Take courage. I am here!" ²⁸Then Peter called to him, "Lord, if it's really you, tell me to come to you, walking on the water." ²⁹"Yes, come," Jesus said. So Peter went over the side of the boat and walked on the water toward Jesus. ³⁰But when he saw the strong wind and the waves, he was terrified and began to sink. "Save me, Lord!" he shouted. ³¹Jesus immediately reached out and grabbed him. "You have so little faith," Jesus said. "Why did you doubt me?"

Be the first to step out on faith. Peter first believed what Jesus told him he could do and walked on water with Jesus; however, be began to doubt it was possible and he began to sink. You should never doubt what God says He will do for you and you should obey his every word. Don't wait on other folks' approval when you know God is telling you to do something.

2. Focus on your future. Never focus on your past. It will depress you! Try to break out of the cycle of your past. Even if you've had a good past, it's over. A troubled past can be an indication of how great your future will be. The devil will always do things

to you or remind you of your past to keep you from focusing on your future.

> **Psalms 66:8-12 (NLT)** 8 Let the whole world bless our God and loudly sing his praises. 9 Our lives are in his hands, and he keeps our feet from stumbling. 10 You have tested us, O God; you have purified us like silver. 11 You captured us in your net and laid the burden of slavery on our backs. 12 Then you put a leader over us. We went through fire and flood, but you brought us to a place of great abundance.

3. Factor in favor. God's favor can take you further than any asset you think you currently have. God's favor can bless you when the odds are against you. God's favor can give you ownership when your credit score is low. (I'll talk more about favor later)

You should prepare your family for the future battles you must face. Be prepared to win as a family. You must show your family the leadership it needs and not run from the fights of your life. The Lord spoke to Joshua about leading his people after Moses died.

> **Joshua 1:7-9 (NLT)** 7Be strong and very courageous. Be careful to obey all the instructions Moses gave you. Do not

> deviate from them, turning either to the right or to the left. Then you will be successful in everything you do. [8]Study this Book of Instruction continually. Meditate on it day and night so you will be sure to obey everything written in it. Only then will you prosper and succeed in all you do. [9]This is my command—be strong and courageous! Do not be afraid or discouraged. For the LORD your God is with you wherever you go."

Tell your family they must look to God for strength to live their daily lives. Tell them how God's love will never fail them, regardless of the perils they face. You must first believe this yourself.

> **Romans 8:38-39 (NLT)** [38]And I am convinced that nothing can ever separate us from God's love. Neither death nor life, neither angels nor demons, neither our fears for today nor our worries about tomorrow—not even the powers of hell can separate us from God's love. [39]No power in the sky above or in the earth below—indeed, nothing in all creation will ever be able to separate us from the love of God that is revealed in Christ Jesus our Lord.

There is so much going on in families these days that it's hard to believe God is still there taking care of you. Don't give up the hope that God will bless you. As I've been told before, you do what you can and let God take care of the rest. Just because things aren't happening at the times you want them to, it does not mean God is not working things out for you. Be prepared to move from a place of not enough to just enough; then from just enough to plenty (more than enough).

> **Jeremiah 29:11-13 (NLT)** [11]For I know the plans I have for you," says the LORD. "They are plans for good and not for disaster, to give you a future and a hope. [12]In those days when you pray, I will listen. [13]If you look for me wholeheartedly, you will find me.

Look to God to fulfill your hopes and dreams. God will give you what you dream of. After all, many of the positive dreams we have were inspired by God to show you things He wants for you. God has planned greatness for your family as well so be prepared to win as I said before. I have learned in the past that winning starts with the things within you.

> **Hebrews 9:14-15 (NLT)** [14]Just think how much more the blood of Christ will

> purify our consciences from sinful deeds so that we can worship the living God. For by the power of the eternal Spirit, Christ offered himself to God as a perfect sacrifice for our sins. [15]That is why he is the one who mediates a new covenant between God and people, so that all who are called can receive the eternal inheritance God has promised them. For Christ died to set them free from the penalty of the sins they had committed under that first covenant.

After you look to Christ for answers, seize the moment when you know it's time to move. You must be willing to move from your comfort zone. You and your family should set short term goals, intermediate goals, and long-term goals. After that, be ready to fight!

Empowered By Wisdom

Power to Deal with Life's Problems

The longer we live, the more problems we will have experienced! Problems come and go no matter what your educational level or how much money you make. Vaughn discussed this in his book when he made references to former presidential candidate Dan Quayle. Quayle caught a lot of flak from the public for speaking his opinion on the problem with families in the United States. "Quayle said that children need love and discipline; that they need mothers and fathers. He said that a welfare check is not a husband, that the state is not a father. He said that marriage is probably the best antipoverty program of all, because only 5.7% of families headed by married couples are in poverty, while 33.4% of families headed by a single mother are in poverty." "Where there are no mature, responsible men around to teach boys how to become good men," Dan Quayle said, "gangs serve in their place. In fact, gangs have become a surrogate family for much of a generation of inner city boys."

There are biblical principles that play a role here. Ephesians 5 says that the husband must love his wife, and that the wife must respect her husband. Vaughn asked, "What would cause a man not to love his wife? Nagging. Lack of respect from his wife. Lies. His wife doesn't listen to him. She gives more affection and time to others than to him. A wife who won't communicate. A wife who doesn't respect herself. An untidy wife. A sneaky wife. A wife who competes with her husband. A wife who won't boost his ego. Being treated like a child. A wife who is very moody and always crying. A wife who is contradictory and argumentative. A wife who manipulates. A wife who is critical and untrustworthy. A wife who talks down to her husband. All these things are examples of needs not being met."

"Time brings about changes, age brings about changes, and we have to grow together in order to know who each other is. But, when we believe that we know everything about our mate, our mate will eventually become boring to us and it's easy to become attracted to someone else. We need to learn how to be there for each other."

Matthew 23:11-12 tells us the greatest among you must be a servant. But those who exalt themselves will be humbled, and those who humble themselves will be exalted. Vaughn said, "In marriage, it should be mutual giving and mutual serving. The husband should have the same kind of servant's attitude as his wife has. But in a lot of relationship, there isn't mutual giving. We think of husband and wife sharing the load 50/50. Sometimes it may be 80/20, and the person who's giving 80% finds that it starts to wear on him or her. If you're always the one to apologize, eventually this thing will bother you."

Someone said listening is a lost art today. Many of us are so concerned about expressing what we think or believe that we just don't listen closely to others - or even to God. As a Christian, try to develop your senses so that you can hear God's voice in the midst of the world's noise. God speaks not only through the Bible, but also through godly counsel and His Holy Spirit. If you want to know what God desires for you, just ask Him. But then be ready to listen for His answer. All it takes is a simple prayer like the one

Empowered By Wisdom

Samuel prayed in 1 Samuel 3:10, where he said to God, "I am listening." You never know just how God will speak to you, so listen for His still, small voice to answer.

Listening to your spouse is important in marriage. Vaughn said, "You need to recognize that marriage is something you have to work at. The work never stops. Both individuals should have a strong commitment to making their marriage work. Both of you have to have a heart of forgiveness. Both of you need to realize that you are going to have bad times. You should be ready for them, and expect them."

You must get in place to be blessed. This means you must accept visions God gives you and seek it out despite what your circumstances might be. You must have the wisdom of how to deal with fools. Proverbs 23:9 says don't waste your breath on fools, for they will despise the wisest advice. Be wise enough to seek the truth from your situations. Proverbs 23:23 says to get the truth and never sell it; also get wisdom, discipline, and good judgment.

I found out through training on my job that a person has to become "resilient" in dealing with life's problems. Resilience: "Is the ability to withstand, recover and/or grow in the face of stressors and changing demands." (DCoE, 2014)

This means that you have to:

1. You have to learn to lean on friends, family, and sometimes coworkers for support.
2. You must learn to take responsibility

Empowered By Wisdom

3. You must use positive and empowering attitudes
4. You have to bounce back, move ahead and forward from problems

You must also develop a positive orientation in your life's outlook:

1. Focus upon positives such as gratitude, blessings, delights, interests, and love
2. Cope with hard times through laughter, humor and fun!
3. Make time to play & have fun!
4. Increase contacts and support from important people in your life, such as good coworkers

You should avoid reaching dead ends:

1. Avoid unpleasant memories, thoughts, and feelings
2. Repress negative feelings
3. Negatives tend to keep you stuck and make it difficult to rebound

In order to move ahead and reach success, you must:

1. Focus on the future rather than dwell on past
2. Not become preoccupied and stuck in the past or you will be unable to move on.
3. Learn from what you've gone through.
4. Look ahead and plan for the next steps.

This all means that you have to get in place to get your blessing from God. In the book, "So You Call Youself a Man?" by T.D. Jakes, Jakes said, "There are some things that God has planned to do, has made provision for doing, and desires to do that He will not do until man is in place to receive what God intends to give." (Jakes, 2007)

"There are some things God has in the heavenlies that will not be released to you until you are in the proper position spiritually, relationally, emotionally. You have an inner knowing that you aren't fully where you ought to be. You have an uneasiness, a frustration that causes you to say, "Why am I no further than this in my life?" Rather than blaming your wife, your parents, your boss, or your race… you are wise to ask yourself, "Is God waiting on me to be in a different spiritual position before He pours out a blessing on my life? When you are in alignment with God and His purposes, He *will* open up the heavens and cause it to RAIN on you! You'll experience such an outpouring of God's blessings that you won't know how to contain them."

T.D. Jakes refers to what he calls "get-over" spirit. "So often we approach people the same way this lame man did. We are looking for what they are going to do for us. We are looking for what we can get from them. We aren't looking for what it is that God wants to do in us or through us. The person with a get-over spirit is always looking for some one or some thing to help him get over his problem. He's looking for what he can take from others, or what they will give to him freely without any effort or responsibility on his part. People with a get-over spirit are users. They use people, but don't really love them. They latch onto people and seek to take from them what they desire or lust after – it may be sex, it may be money, it may be fawning adoration. They have little interest in other people apart from what they can get from them that will help them make it from today to tomorrow."

Some of you may think this applies only to people who don't have anything or don't have money. Jakes said, "Now you don't have to be poor or financially destitute to have a get-over spirit. You can be rich and still blame your problems on somebody else who you believe is failing to do for you what you think they should be doing for you. You may be a very wealthy business owner and still have a get-over attitude, blaming your employees or your competitors for keeping you from your success you think you should have. You can be a church pastor and have a get-over attitude, blaming the members of your church for not appreciating you the way you think you should be appreciated."

I agree with Jakes when he said, "Nobody can be your Source but God. And nobody can put you into a right relationship with God but you." Kirk Franklin said it succinctly when you said, "we need to stop teaching religion and start teaching relationships."

We must be Spiritually Secure! Spiritual Security empowers us to excel during devastating times. We must guard our hearts and minds. There are built-in alarms that we should listen to. In the physical sense, we have all sorts of alarms and security systems. Jakes said, "While this is true for material possessions, so many men do not have a security system for their emotional and spiritual lives. Part of the reason is that they don't know *they* are valuable to God. And another part of the reason is that they don't know that a thief is loose in the world who wants to steal, destroy, and kill everything of value that they possess."

We must know what we are fighting for and against! Jakes said, "... the man who gets up every day knowing who he is battling is a man who can fight with purpose and intelligence and direction. In order to win you must know that God is the Source of your life and that you have an enemy of your eternal spirit, and that God your Source will help you defeat your enemy. It is only when you come to that awareness that life makes sense."

You must get strength from God and be willing to step forward and fight! Jakes said, "Don't expect God to speak up for you – or to cause others to see you for who you really are – until you are willing to step into the place where God has called you to be. When you step into that place where you are supposed to be, you don't have to speak up for yourself, fight for yourself, or demand anything of others. God will speak for you. He'll command whatever forces are involved to yield to you, give to you, honor you, listen to you, obey you. Don't expect God to open up the heavens and pour out His Spirit of power and truth and wisdom and righteousness onto your life unless you are where you are supposed to be."

In order to be in the right place you have to be of the right mind and spirit! Jakes said, "You cannot be the head of your house and be hysterical at the same time. You can't fall apart just because your wife has fallen apart. You can't lose your cool just because your kids have lost theirs. Somebody has to keep their wits about them and say, "We're going to come out of this." As priests of your home, you are called to be a stabilizing, protecting force in your home. When you walk in the front door of your house, everybody in your family should feel safer. You are called by God to have a "right mind." Let this mind be in you, which was also in Christ Jesus" (Philippians 2:5).

Jakes added that, "Having a right mind means being aware of your responsibilities and accepting them. I know many men who let their wives deal with all the stress of the family, including anxiety over the family finances, worries over the spiritual life of each family member, and concerns over family provision. That's not her role. You and your wife must share the responsibility for your children and work together to make a plan for your family."

The contemporary Christian artist group 4Him sings a song called, Measure of a Man. "The measure of a man is not how tall he stands, how wealthy, or intelligent you are." They later sing, "What's in the heart defines the measure of a man." They also sing, "There is more to what's you're worth than human eyes can see." The lyrics to this song are so prophetic and you should take it to heart as I did.

A man's worth should not be measured by what he has. We live in a very materialistic society. Don't get mixed up in the confusion of placing value in the wrong places. The things that God bless you to obtain should never replace him as your God. That includes fame, money, cars, houses, and even people.

It's time for you to come out of the shadows as a Christian. R&B artist India Arie in her song, "Strength, Courage, and Wisdom", said "you have to step out on faith, it's time to show my face." When you step into the light of the Lord, people will notice you even though their responses won't always be positive. Indie Arie in her song, "There's Hope", said, "It doesn't cost a thing to smile, you don't have to pay to laugh, you better thank God for that." India Arie in her song, "I Choose", said, "I choose to the best that I can be, I choose to be authentic in everything I do. My past don't dictate who I am, I choose." "Because you never know where life is going to take you and you can't change where you've been, but today I have the opportunity to choose." You have a choice to be all that God called you to be.

Men, it's time for us to treat the women in our lives better! India Arie said, "I See God in You". You should not have to daily shout out to the world to let them know you are a Christian. The way you walk, talk, and act should show them you are different. Have the wisdom to know living the life of a believer is better than shouting it out to everyone. Anyone can claim to be a Christian or anything else. It is better for people to see what you're about as you're living the example. India Arie in the song, "Can I Walk With You", said, "you make me feel like I can be a better woman, if you just say you want to take this friendship to another place, can I walk with you in your life, can I lay with you as your wife. Can I be your friend to the end, can I walk with you through your life."

The words that come to mind now is commitment. We must not be afraid to commit ourselves to one woman and our own family. Nicole C. Mullen in her song, "The Ring", said, "If you wanna step to me, you better know one thang, this love I got you'll never get without a wedding ring."

Vickie Winans, in her song, "I Promise", said, "Now the intimacy between two lovers is so special, but reserved for married people, so I promise to wait for that someone special set aside for me, until the day I say, I do."

This all is again a matter of faith. Faith is one of the most important things God demands from us. We can now talk about faith in future grace compared to impatience. I have learned that we must have a passion for God's glory. The book of John talked about patience and endurance.

> **James 5:7-11 (NLT)** [7]Dear brothers and sisters, be patient as you wait for the Lord's return. Consider the farmers who patiently wait for the rains in the fall and in the spring. They eagerly look for the valuable harvest to ripen. [8]You, too, must be patient. Take courage, for the coming of the Lord is near. [9]Don't grumble about each other, brothers and sisters, or you will be judged. For look—the Judge is standing at the door! [10]For examples of patience in suffering, dear brothers and sisters, look at the prophets who spoke in the name of the Lord. [11]We give great honor to those who endure under suffering. For instance, you know about Job, a man of great endurance. You can see how the Lord was kind to him at the end, for the Lord is full of tenderness and mercy.

Empowered By Wisdom

I must admit that life challenges our patience, but this is normal. In the midst of our problems, you should be aware of God's reign. Our faith is strengthened by patience. I believe impatience is a form of unbelief. On the other hand, patience is the ability to wait and endure; without complaining, grumbling, pouting or being disillusioned. Patience is a mark of spiritual strength. 2 Corinthians 4:16-18 reminds us of an eternal perspective.

> **2 Corinthians 4:16 - 18 (NLT)** [16]That is why we never give up. Though our bodies are dying, our spirits are being renewed every day. [17]For our present troubles are small and won't last very long. Yet they produce for us a glory that vastly outweighs them and will last forever! [18]So we don't look at the troubles we can see now; rather, we fix our gaze on things that cannot be seen. For the things we see now will soon be gone, but the things we cannot see will last forever.

Paul prayed for the church at Colossae, that they would be "strengthened and all power according to His glorious might, for the attaining of all steadfastness and patience" (Colossians 1:11).

I learned while I was in Afghanistan that faith is the channel to transform barriers. Faith gives us the strength to endure hardships. The strength of patience hangs on our capacity to believe that God is up to something good for us. God has promised again and again in the Bible to turn all things for the good of his people (2 Chronicles 16:9; Psalm 23:6, 84:11; Jeremiah 32:40-41; Isaiah 64:4; Romans 8:28, 32: 1 Corinthians 3:22-23). John Piper said the Key to Patience: "God meant it for good". (Piper, 2005)

Genesis 37-50 tells the story of Joseph. Joseph was a good example of having patience. Many of the things that has happened and will happen in our lives were unplanned, but God had His hands in it all along. Piper said grace is coming in future grace – the sovereign grace of God to turn the unplanned place and the unplanned pace into the happiest ending imaginable. James commands us to be patient and gives us the key in James 5:7-11. God's goal is for us to see his compassion and mercy. (Piper, 2005)

There is a difference between faith in future grace and covetousness.

> **1 Timothy 6:6-12 (NLT)** [6]Yet true godliness with contentment is itself great wealth. [7]After all, we brought nothing with us when we came into the world, and we can't take anything with us when we leave it. [8]So if we have enough food and clothing, let us be content. [9]But people who long to be rich fall into temptation and are trapped by many foolish and harmful desires that plunge

> them into ruin and destruction. ¹⁰For the love of money is the root of all kinds of evil. And some people, craving money, have wandered from the true faith and pierced themselves with many sorrows. ¹¹But you, Timothy, are a man of God; so run from all these evil things. Pursue righteousness and a godly life, along with faith, love, perseverance, and gentleness. ¹²Fight the good fight for the true faith. Hold tightly to the eternal life to which God has called you, which you have confessed so well before many witnesses.

Covetousness is desiring something so much that you lose your contentment in God. It is a form of idolatry. Forbidden in the Ten Commandments: "You shall have no other gods before me" (Exod. 20:3) and "You shall not covet" (Exod. 20:17). Contentment in God is faith in God. 1 Tim 6:6-12 indicates the goal is to be godly and content in God. A key is to flee the love of money and desire to be rich (verse 11). This is a constant fight for faith (verse 12) to flee covetousness.

Paul says this fight is also a secret (Philippians 4:11-12). The secret is 4:13 "I can do all things through him. All I need to do is glorify God. Piper gave Five Warnings for fighting covetousness:

- Covetousness never brings satisfaction. Ecc. 5:10, Luke 12:15

Empowered By Wisdom

- Covetousness chokes off the spiritual life. Parable of the soils (Mark 4:1-20), some seed "fell among the thorns, ...and choked it." The thorns are: "the worries of the world, and the deceitfulness of riches, and the desires for other things (v. 19).

- Covetousness spawns many other sins. Paul says, "The love of money is the root of all evils." 1 Tim 6:10, James 4:2

- Covetousness lets you down when you need help most. 1 Tim 6:7

- In the end covetousness destroys the soul. 1 Tim 6:9

You have nowhere to run but to God. I recommend you pray for a new appetite for God and his word.

> **Psalms 119:36 (NLT)** 36 Give me an eagerness for your laws rather than a love for money!

Remind yourself of the goal: godliness with contentment produces great gain (1 Tim 6:6). Hold to God's promises and keep your lives free from the love of money and be content... God has said (promises), "Never will I leave you; never will I forsake you... The Lord is my helper; I will not be afraid."

Empowered By Wisdom

Life presents many challenges. Living your life as a Christian does not excuse you from having to face stress. It's time to learn how to pass the stress test.

> **James 1:2-8 (NLT)** ²Dear brothers and sisters, when troubles come your way, consider it an opportunity for great joy. ³For you know that when your faith is tested, your endurance has a chance to grow. ⁴So let it grow, for when your endurance is fully developed, you will be perfect and complete, needing nothing. ⁵If you need wisdom, ask our generous God, and he will give it to you. He will not rebuke you for asking. ⁶But when you ask him, be sure that your faith is in God alone. Do not waver, for a person with divided loyalty is as unsettled as a wave of the sea that is blown and tossed by the wind. ⁷Such people should not expect to receive anything from the Lord. ⁸Their loyalty is divided between God and the world, and they are unstable in everything they do.

Devotion to God's words and showing true faith will get you further in life than any amount of money, fame, or fortune. None of us are immune to temptation for we are imperfect creature made from a perfect being.

> **James 1:12 - 15 (NLT)** [12]God blesses those who patiently endure testing and temptation. Afterward they will receive the crown of life that God has promised to those who love him. [13]And remember, when you are being tempted, do not say, "God is tempting me." God is never tempted to do wrong, and he never tempts anyone else. [14]Temptation comes from our own desires, which entice us and drag us away. [15]These desires give birth to sinful actions. And when sin is allowed to grow, it gives birth to death.

We were made in God's image and we can count on His spirit that lives within us. When the tests come or when temptation becomes overwhelming, we must turn to God for help. Although God will place good people we can turn to in our lives, no one can comfort and guide you like the Lord.

> **Ephesians 3:20 (NLT)** [20]Now all glory to God, who is able, through his mighty power at work within us, to accomplish infinitely more than we might ask or think.

Faith prepares us to deal with the difficulty of life. Some of us associate stress with trying to make enough money to take care of ourselves, family, and the bills, and possibly save some. However, even people with money have to deal with stress on a different level. Having money does not excuse you from having stress. No matter your financial situation, only God can give you peace of mind. The more you give your life to God, the more the devil will stress you. I have found that through living life, stress is predictable and unavoidable. You have to learn how to face stress. John 16:33 tells us to be of good cheer.

1 Peter 4:12 tells us to not be concerns about the trials around us. The saying goes, the greater the trial, the greater the victory. We must know our battle is already won so let the stress go. Stress left unchecked will become explosive! Don't let stress catch you off guard. When it comes to your problems and experiences, count it all joy. Have the faith to know God is there for you and will see you through. Faith is the power internally to deal with problems externally. Sometimes trials come with a purpose of correction and perfection.

You must stay in the fight for your life! Don't let the devil wear you out. Weariness will bring fear to your life. Weariness can hinder prayer. Don't let anything hinder your prayer life. Trials are designed by the enemy to take you away from God. Don't let anger get the best of you. If you're going to lose your temper, lose it on the devil. Being worn out means mental wearing out and exhaustion.

The danger signals of being worn down are fatigue, exhaustion, tiredness, and a lack of vitality. To disarm the devil, you have to put on the whole armor of God. We have to develop a combat faith and prepare to fight against the enemy. God wants to invade every aspect of our lives, even our hobbies. As God is taking us from level to level, he's also taking us from glory to glory. Life is a series of beginning again.

> **Philippians 1:6 (NLT)** 6And I am certain that God, who began the good work within you, will continue his work until it is finally finished on the day when Christ Jesus returns.

Now that you know God is on your side, begin to prepare for prosperity. Practice getting excited about something you haven't received yet. Develop your life with a sense of urgency. Lighten up with concerns about your problems or limitations. One way the devil wears us out is placing things heavily on your mind. Mental stress can cause physical tiredness.

> **Revelation 3:8 (NLT)** 8"I know all the things you do, and I have opened a door for you that no one can close. You have little strength, yet you obeyed my word and did not deny me.

Sometimes your problems can seem bigger than what you can stand. You may feel hopeless; however, there is always hope in God. Even though his timing is not our timing, he'll always be right on time to deliver us. Our problem is we get so used to living in our problem that there appears to be no way out. No matter how grim things look for you, God will bring you out!

> **Psalms 68:9-10 (NLT)** ⁹ You sent abundant rain, O God, to refresh the weary land. ¹⁰ There your people finally settled, and with a bountiful harvest, O God, you provided for your needy people.

Some of you are concerned with your health or the health of a love one. Remember this, God still heals! You must realize that God can heal through medicine, healing, and your worship. You don't need to worry if you're faithful in God's word. Sometimes things may not turn out the way you wanted but God's still working things out for your good.

> **Zephaniah 3:17 (NLT)** ¹⁷ For the LORD your God is living among you. He is a mighty savior. He will take delight in you with gladness. With his love, he will calm all your fears. He will rejoice over you with joyful songs."

Empowered By Wisdom

There are things that block us from healing:

- Unbelief – above all else, we must believe in the power of God. None of the things I have said will do you any good unless you believe.

- Unforgiveness – we must purge ourselves of any unforgiveness. Who are you to ask God for forgiveness and you can't forgive your fellow man?

- Personal sins – repeated personal sins are a problem! God will forgive us for our sins but that does not mean we should keep committing the same sine. Ask God for strength to overcome your sinful nature.

- Wrong focus – We have a tendency to seek after the wrong people and go for the wrong things. What we need to do is keep our eyes on Jesus! He will lead us to good things!

> **Psalms 91:14-16 (NLT)** [14] The LORD says, "I will rescue those who love me. I will protect those who trust in my name. [15] When they call on me, I will answer; I will be with them in trouble. I will rescue and honor them. [16] I will reward them with a long life and give them my salvation."

Throughout life there are many things we have to go through. There will be many decisions to make and countless paths to take. Unfortunately, as a consequence to making bad decisions, we have to suffer and end up regretting these decisions and circumstances. Don't let regret drag you down spiritually.

Regret is a form of condemnation. There are regrets in family, finances, decisions, and bad habits. Some Christians punish themselves with "If only.." You can't keep reaching back to old mistakes and pulling them into your present. Since we are weak and broken down, God has to do some divine repair on us.

> **2 Corinthians 7:8-10 (NLT)** [8] I am not sorry that I sent that severe letter to you, though I was sorry at first, for I know it was painful to you for a little while. [9] Now I am glad I sent it, not because it hurt you, but because the pain caused you to repent and change your ways. It was the kind of sorrow God wants his people to have, so you were not harmed by us in any way. [10] For the kind of sorrow God wants us to experience leads us away from sin and results in salvation. There's no regret for that kind of sorrow. But worldly sorrow, which lacks repentance, results in spiritual death.

There are some things in life you have to get over! Have the wisdom to know regret pollutes your faith. We need to discuss what we usually do with regret, what we should do, and what God wants us to do. To cover it all, God wants us to turn to Him.

There are ways to let go of your regrets:

1. Bury them – minimize, rationalize
- We can compromise (lower standards)
- We can blame others – accused and excused
- We can beat ourselves down

> **Psalms 38:4-8 (NLT)** 4 My guilt overwhelms me— it is a burden too heavy to bear. 5 My wounds fester and stink because of my foolish sins. 6 I am bent over and racked with pain. All day long I walk around filled with grief. 7 A raging fever burns within me, and my health is broken. 8 I am exhausted and completely crushed. My groans come from an anguished heart.

2. Admit your guilt. One of the first things we do as humans related to problems we face is to deny there is a problem. The next is admitting your part in the problem. Confess all your sins to God and ask Him for help with them.

> **Psalms 32:5 (NLT)** ⁵ Finally, I confessed all my sins to you and stopped trying to hide my guilt. I said to myself, "I will confess my rebellion to the LORD." And you forgave me! All my guilt is gone.

3. Accept God's forgiveness. As always, God will forgive our sins. Our problems had its purposes but it's time to move on.

> **Isaiah 38:16-17 (NLT)** ¹⁶ Lord, your discipline is good, for it leads to life and health. You restore my health and allow me to live! ¹⁷ Yes, this anguish was good for me, for you have rescued me from death and forgiven all my sins.

4. Forgive yourself and focus on future. Even after God forgives our sins, we must forgive ourselves. There's not much worse than the regret from things that happen to us based on our own actions. Get over it! Now is the time for focusing on the positive things God has for you in the future.

> **Isaiah 43:18-19 (NLT)** ¹⁸ "But forget all that— it is nothing compared to what I am going to do. ¹⁹ For I am about to do something new. See, I have already

> begun! Do you not see it? I will make a pathway through the wilderness. I will create rivers in the dry wasteland.

5. Clear your conscience. The devil will continue to try to get you in your thoughts. Contrary to popular belief, just because you thought of something, it does not mean that's the kind of person you are nor should you do everything you think of. Distance yourself from the way you used to think, act, or talk.

> **Jeremiah 31:34 (NLT)** [34]And they will not need to teach their neighbors, nor will they need to teach their relatives, saying, 'You should know the LORD.' For everyone, from the least to the greatest, will know me already," says the LORD. "And I will forgive their wickedness, and I will never again remember their sins."

Remember, God chooses to forget your sin but you have to change your character. You can't remain the same after you have truly experienced God. Jesus was nailed to the cross so you won't have to nail yourself.

All too often we focus on how little we have when it comes to things God place on our minds to do. God can turn your little into a lot!

Mark 6:35 - 44 (NLT) [35]Late in the afternoon his disciples came to him and said, "This is a remote place, and it's already getting late. [36]Send the crowds away so they can go to the nearby farms and villages and buy something to eat." [37]But Jesus said, "You feed them." "With what?" they asked. "We'd have to work for months to earn enough money to buy food for all these people!" [38]"How much bread do you have?" he asked. "Go and find out." They came back and reported, "We have five loaves of bread and two fish." [39]Then Jesus told the disciples to have the people sit down in groups on the green grass. [40]So they sat down in groups of fifty or a hundred. [41]Jesus took the five loaves and two fish, looked up toward heaven, and blessed them. Then, breaking the loaves into pieces, he kept giving the bread to the disciples so they could distribute it to the people. He also divided the fish for everyone to share. [42]They all ate as much as they wanted, [43]and afterward, the disciples picked up twelve baskets of leftover bread and fish. [44]A total of 5,000 men and their families were fed from those loaves!

Empowered By Wisdom

The same story was repeated in John 6:7, 9. The moral of these stories is that God can do anything. There is nothing too big that God can do for you or through you. There are three things a person must do before expecting a miracle:

1. Identify the problem/need

2. Accept responsibility for problem

3. Make sure you do what you can

God sees all your problems. In order to progress, you have to recognize the problem first. There are three ways to handle a problem:

1. Don't procrastinate

2. Don't pass the buck

3. Don't give up

God tests you in different ways in your spiritual life. You must try to be strong. Sometimes following God might mean standing alone. That's alright for you can make it! Sometimes, God will test us physically. Pray for strength to endure.

> **Luke 4:1-4 (NLT)** [1] Then Jesus, full of the Holy Spirit, returned from the Jordan River. He was led by the Spirit in the wilderness, [2] where he was tempted by the devil for forty days. Jesus ate nothing

> all that time and became very hungry. ³Then the devil said to him, "If you are the Son of God, change this stone into a loaf of bread." ⁴But Jesus told him, "No! The Scriptures say, 'People do not live by bread alone.'"

This story is not really about the bread. The story is about how the devil will try to convince you to prove God is real in some form of public display. Don't ever feel you have to prove to the devil or anyone else that God is real and can bless you.

> **Luke 4:12-13 (NLT)** ¹²Jesus responded, "The Scriptures also say, 'You must not test the LORD your God.'" ¹³When the devil had finished tempting Jesus, he left him until the next opportunity came.

The path to power is by testing. God wants to see where your true faith and allegiance lie. Trust in the Lord and do all that he tells you to do. Leave everything else to God. God can do things that are humanly impossible.

> **Jeremiah 32:17 (NLT)** ¹⁷"O Sovereign LORD! You made the heavens and earth

> by your strong hand and powerful arm.
> Nothing is too hard for you!

Do what you can with what you have and expect God to do the rest. Have faith enough to know that you can ask God for something and if it's in His will, you can have it. Did you know that with the right amount of faith, you get to choose how much God will do in your life?

> **Matthew 9:27 - 29 (NLT)** ²⁷After Jesus left the girl's home, two blind men followed along behind him, shouting, "Son of David, have mercy on us!" ²⁸They went right into the house where he was staying, and Jesus asked them, "Do you believe I can make you see?" "Yes, Lord," they told him, "we do." ²⁹Then he touched their eyes and said, "Because of your faith, it will happen."

Sometimes when we're blessed with money, we think we show ourselves powerful by giving lots of money to charities or by funding certain events. You can never out-give God. When put in the right perspective, God can use you to be a blessing to others. Look for these opportunities but watch your motives for what you do. God loves doing miracles through people.

Empowered By Wisdom

Why We Must Have Wisdom

I believe God wants His children to be different than worldly people. When we use and apply Godly wisdom to our worldly situations, we would appear differently than others.
Exodus 28:2 - 3 asked the people of Israel to make sacred garments for Aaron that were glorious and beautiful. They were to instruct all the skilled craftsmen whom God filled with the spirit of wisdom. He had them make garments for Aaron that will distinguish him as a priest set apart for God's service.

God sometimes chooses certain people to stand out among others. In Exodus 31:1 – 5, God told Moses that He specifically chose Bezalel son of Uri, grandson of Hur, of the tribe of Judah, and filled him with the Spirit of God, giving him great wisdom, ability, and expertise in all kinds of crafts. Bezalel was a master craftsman, expert in working with gold, silver, and bronze. God wanted Bezalel to do something special in God's name. In your quest for wisdom, God may call on you to lead others whether it be in a church or on your job. The bible speaks of this in Deuteronomy. Moses was speaking to the people of Israel and complained about not being able to carry all of them by himself. In Deuteronomy 1:13, Moses told the people of Israel, to choose some well-respected men from each tribe who are known for their wisdom and understanding, and he will appoint them as their leaders.

When you're trying to find wisdom, have you ever considered the wisdom of God? There is a difference between man's wisdom and God's wisdom. Proverbs 4:5 tells us the importance of wisdom.

> **Proverbs 4:5 (NLT)** Get wisdom; develop good judgment. Don't forget my words or turn away from them.

Man's wisdom is not as good as God's wisdom.

> **1 Corinthians 2:4-7 (NLT)** [4]And my message and my preaching were very plain. Rather than using clever and persuasive speeches, I relied only on the power of the Holy Spirit. [5]I did this so you would trust not in human wisdom but in the power of God. [6]Yet when I am among mature believers, I do speak with words of wisdom, but not the kind of wisdom that belongs to this world or to the rulers of this world, who are soon forgotten. [7]No, the wisdom we speak of is the mystery of God—his plan that was previously hidden, even though he made it for our ultimate glory before the world began.

God's wisdom surpasses any other wisdom there may be.

Empowered By Wisdom

> **1 Corinthians 1:18 - 20 (NLT)** [18]The message of the cross is foolish to those who are headed for destruction! But we who are being saved know it is the very power of God. [19]As the Scriptures say, "I will destroy the wisdom of the wise and discard the intelligence of the intelligent." [20]So where does this leave the philosophers, the scholars, and the world's brilliant debaters? God has made the wisdom of this world look foolish.

When we are trying to get away from worldly wisdom we must understand the different parts of ourselves. The Natural man is a person (like Nicodemus) that's not saved. A Carnal man as discussed in 1 Cor 3 is a person that is saved but think and act like the world. Lastly, the Spiritual man is one who is led by the spirit (word of God).

> **1 Corinthians 3:18 - 19 (NLT)** [18]Stop deceiving yourselves. If you think you are wise by this world's standards, you need to become a fool to be truly wise. [19]For the wisdom of this world is foolishness to God. As the Scriptures say, "He traps the wise in the snare of their own cleverness."

Empowered By Wisdom

I learned some time ago that God's goodness and mercy cannot be superseded. He brought us from Egypt (Bondage) to the Wilderness (Salvation) to the Promise land (Sanctification) to Relief (Blessing).

> **Psalms 119:105 (NLT)** 105 Your word is a lamp to guide my feet and a light for my path.

Proverbs 3:5 says to, "Trust in the LORD with all your heart; do not depend on your own understanding." Natural wisdom will speak to your head, God's wisdom will speak to your heart.

The scripture found in James 3:13-17 sums it all up:

> **James 3:13-17 (NLT)** 13If you are wise and understand God's ways, prove it by living an honorable life, doing good works with the humility that comes from wisdom. 14But if you are bitterly jealous and there is selfish ambition in your heart, don't cover up the truth with boasting and lying. 15For jealousy and selfishness are not God's kind of wisdom. Such things are earthly, unspiritual, and demonic. 16For wherever there is jealousy and selfish ambition, there you will find disorder and evil of

every kind. [17]But the wisdom from above is first of all pure. It is also peace loving, gentle at all times, and willing to yield to others. It is full of mercy and good deeds. It shows no favoritism and is always sincere.

Empowered By Wisdom

The Power of God's Word

As believers, we must give God the credit for what he does for us! Even when things aren't going your way, you should realize God is in control and give him praise. God will show up where there's praise! Praise enables anointing – beyond who you are.

> **Psalms 138:2-3 (NLT)** ² I bow before your holy Temple as I worship. I praise your name for your unfailing love and faithfulness; for your promises are backed by all the honor of your name. ³ As soon as I pray, you answer me; you encourage me by giving me strength.

You should rely on the Lord's strength and not just your own.

> **Zechariah 4:6 (NLT)** ⁶Then he said to me, "This is what the LORD says to Zerubbabel: It is not by force nor by strength, but by my Spirit, says the LORD of Heaven's Armies.

Nehemiah was responsible for building a wall. He followed God's orders to build the wall. I bet many people thought Nehemiah was crazy and talked badly about him. When you do the will of God, people will talk badly about you as well. Regardless of how bad people talk about you or mistreat you, you must try to get along with them in peace. It's very important to have unity in your family and your community.

> **Psalms 133:1 (NLT)** ¹ How wonderful and pleasant it is when brothers live together in harmony!

There must be the order in your family, job, and community as God demanded. You must bring them the word with understanding. Following God's word will guide you to do the right things.

> **Psalms 119:29-32 (NLT)** ²⁹ Keep me from lying to myself; give me the privilege of knowing your instructions. ³⁰ I have chosen to be faithful; I have determined to live by your regulations. ³¹ I cling to your laws. LORD, don't let me be put to shame! ³² I will pursue your commands, for you expand my understanding.

God's Word gives light and understanding to a dark world. You must be ready for God to shake the bad things out of your life. Are You Ready for the Shaking? I've learned that you should not let people and stuff frustrate you. Realize your security is not in what you have but Who you have. In your salvation, God is altering your mind. Unfortunately, many people aren't listening to God but the philosophy of man. Man will create a cage to keep you in; the intent is to keep you from sharing the joy that only God can give.

Having worked in the military and now working for the military as a civilian, I was aware of a limit the government placed on supervisor about talking about "religion" to subordinates. I just went through respect to religion training recently and they talked about supervisor facilitating varying religious freedoms of their subordinates as well their right to not have a faith system at all. Being a Christian, I have to respect my subordinates' rights; however, I don't think that means I can't be who I am. I have to know what I can say and do and respect my subordinates rights as well, without forcing my beliefs on them.

> **Deuteronomy 4:5-8 (NLT)** [5]"Look, I now teach you these decrees and regulations just as the LORD my God commanded me, so that you may obey them in the land you are about to enter and occupy. [6]Obey them completely, and you will display your wisdom and intelligence among the surrounding nations. When they hear all these decrees, they will exclaim, 'How wise and

> prudent are the people of this great nation!' ⁷For what great nation has a god as near to them as the LORD our God is near to us whenever we call on him? ⁸And what great nation has decrees and regulations as righteous and fair as this body of instructions that I am giving you today?

When you come to God for something, you should know that in His own time, God will not only provide, but He has already provided! Get yourself in order and be ready for a blessing.

> **1 Corinthians 14:33 (NLT)** ³³For God is not a God of disorder but of peace, as in all the meetings of God's holy people.

There's a necessity to get in order. There is a difference between world order and God's order. The problem is, people who don't have order don't plan on going anywhere. Genesis 1 says God called order out of chaos. You must have a teachable heart and you have to be ready for change. Things happen to us all the time. You can't take stuff personally. You have to learn to let your standard be excellence. Be committed to getting things in order, and keeping them in order. If things get out of order, make it your goal to get back in order.

Empowered By Wisdom

Proverbs 4:1-19 (NLT) [1] My children, listen when your father corrects you. Pay attention and learn good judgment, [2] for I am giving you good guidance. Don't turn away from my instructions. [3] For I, too, was once my father's son, tenderly loved as my mother's only child. [4] My father taught me, "Take my words to heart. Follow my commands, and you will live. [5] Get wisdom; develop good judgment. Don't forget my words or turn away from them. [6] Don't turn your back on wisdom, for she will protect you. Love her, and she will guard you. [7] Getting wisdom is the wisest thing you can do! And whatever else you do, develop good judgment. [8] If you prize wisdom, she will make you great. Embrace her, and she will honor you. [9] She will place a lovely wreath on your head; she will present you with a beautiful crown." [10] My child, listen to me and do as I say, and you will have a long, good life. [11] I will teach you wisdom's ways and lead you in straight paths. [12] When you walk, you won't be held back; when you run, you won't stumble. [13] Take hold of my instructions; don't let them go. Guard them, for they are the key to life. [14] Don't do as the wicked do, and don't follow the path of evildoers. [15] Don't even think about it; don't go that way. Turn away and keep moving. ¹⁶ For evil people can't sleep until they've done their evil deed for the day. They can't rest until they've caused someone to stumble. ¹⁷ They eat the food of wickedness and drink the wine of violence! ¹⁸ The way of the righteous is like the first gleam of dawn, which shines ever brighter until the full light of day. ¹⁹ But the way of the wicked is like total darkness. They have no idea what they are stumbling over.

Time to Make a Change

Have wisdom to know it's time to make a change. This may simply mean a change of heart.

> **Ezekiel 36:26-27 (NLT)** [26] And I will give you a new heart, and I will put a new spirit in you. I will take out your stony, stubborn heart and give you a tender, responsive heart. [27] And I will put my Spirit in you so that you will follow my decrees and be careful to obey my regulations.

Growth demands change. We must be willing to make a change within ourselves but remember, God is unchanging. He is always there for you. You should always change for the better. You can't expect to grow if you're unwilling to change. Change is developed by three major components: 1) Challenges, 2) Product of choices, and 3) Taking chances.

You must be willing to step out of your comfort zone. Change is necessary to maximize potential. You should always be willing to do well but don't stop at doing good. Do better than good for good is not good enough. God has ordained us for greatness! I've learned in life to not hang around chickens when you are destined to be an eagle! Good is the biggest hindrance to greatness.

Change has to take place in your heart. What's on the inside governs who you are. When you have a change of heart, you don't worry about what people have to say about you; and they will talk!

> **Proverbs 4:23 (NLT)** 23 Guard your heart above all else, for it determines the course of your life.

Keep your heart right. You should always put your trust in God and love Him with all your heart.

> **John 14:1 (NLT)** 1"Don't let your hearts be troubled. Trust in God, and trust also in me.

Your heart determines your destiny. You must give God your heart and trust the directions He takes you. If you love Him and trust Him, you shouldn't have any trouble doing what He'll have you do. The biggest excuse to not having achieved what God wanted you to do is, "I'm trying". Man's heart is naturally deceitful so that excuse doesn't really justify why you have not done what God wanted you to do.

There are four "I's" to the excuses we make:

1) Inflexible – don't want to bend to God's ways

2) Insensible – will not allow the Spirit of God to touch your heart
3) Irrational – void of understanding
4) Independent – too much "I" in your life
   1. Being independent makes you live an impossible life

Get away from the "I" and learn to depend on God. He will be your protector and your guide.

> **Proverbs 18:10-11 (NLT)** [10] The name of the LORD is a strong fortress; the godly run to him and are safe. [11] The rich think of their wealth as a strong defense; they imagine it to be a high wall of safety.

When you are trying to do the things God want you to do, don't do anything in order to be recognized for what you're doing. Do things for others out of the goodness in your heart and not for the publicity or reward you may get.

> **Proverbs 11:17-19 (NLT)** [17] Your kindness will reward you, but your cruelty will destroy you. [18] Evil people get rich for the moment, but the reward of the godly will last. [19] Godly people find life; evil people find death.

God's word is more powerful than anything you're capable of doing! When you do wrong, you can't hide it from God. Ask God for forgiveness and He will. Thank God for not exposing you when you were doing wrong.

> **Hebrews 4:12 - 13 (NLT)** ¹²For the word of God is alive and powerful. It is sharper than the sharpest two-edged sword, cutting between soul and spirit, between joint and marrow. It exposes our innermost thoughts and desires. ¹³Nothing in all creation is hidden from God. Everything is naked and exposed before his eyes, and he is the one to whom we are accountable.

When you have the Word of God inside, you can never really run from it. When your mind is not right, the Word will pop up. Forget your pride, sin, limitations, and guilt and stand on God's Word. Seek his voice during the storms in your life and He will give you safety and light your path.

> **Luke 8:16-18 (NLT)** ¹⁶ "No one lights a lamp and then covers it with a bowl or hides it under a bed. A lamp is placed on a stand, where its light can be seen by all who enter the house. ¹⁷ For all that is

> secret will eventually be brought into the open, and everything that is concealed will be brought to light and made known to all. [18] "So pay attention to how you hear. To those who listen to my teaching, more understanding will be given. But for those who are not listening, even what they think they understand will be taken away from them."

Like I said initially, it's time to make a change. First of all, you must change the way you see yourself. People don't always see their value to God in themselves. Please don't deny the beauty God has placed inside you. Change involves 3 major factors:

1. Challenge
2. Change is a choice
3. Change involves taking chances
   a) do things you have not done before
   b) you have the ability to change
   c) get away from safe places

I know you feel it's your responsibility to help others; however, change must begin in you. You can't help someone else until you help yourself.

When you become strong in God's power you work towards spiritual authority. Spiritual authority begins with spiritual maturity. Spiritual maturity begins with spiritual identity. You must know who you are as God's child.

Empowered By Wisdom

John 14:6 shows us that Jesus knew who he was:

> **John 14:6 (NLT)** Jesus told him, "I am the way, the truth, and the life. No one can come to the Father except through me.

Do you know who you are? The question is not what people think, but what you think of yourself.

> **Matthew 3:17 (NLT)** And a voice from heaven said, "This is my dearly loved Son, who brings me great joy."

Announcement of Jesus's identity gave him authority.

> **John 1:12-13 (NLT)** 12 But to all who believed him and accepted him, he gave the right to become children of God. 13 They are reborn—not with a physical birth resulting from human passion or plan, but a birth that comes from God.

You were born an original, so don't die a copy. Remember these things:

Empowered By Wisdom

1) You were chosen
2) You're superior on a different level
3) You're holy and set aside
4) You're peculiar and uncommon

You should move from bondage and slavery – the land of not enough. God will make your "not enough" – enough. Just enough is a land of experience. God wants you to move to a land of more than enough. But you must be willing to change.

Three things to change:

1. The land is reserved for VIP's: Change your visualization.

> **Proverbs 23:23 (NLT)** Get the truth and never sell it; also get wisdom, discipline, and good judgment.

2. Change verbalization: Change your language about yourself.

3. Change your salvation: Realize the importance of your giving your life to God.

Pastor Aaron Burke of Radiant Church in Tampa, FL encourages us to Pray First in all we do! I agree with him in that prayer should be used at the beginning of everything and not used as a last resort! We often use prayer when we've done all you can. There's nothing wrong in your taking steps to resolve an issue or problem; however, can you imagine how much more effective you would have been if you'd prayed before you delved into trying to fix the problem? God never promised us we won't have problems but he did tell us will have victory over our problems.

> **Acts 6:3 (NLT)** ³And so, brothers, select seven men who are well respected and are full of the Spirit and wisdom. We will give them this responsibility.

I recommend you recognize the wisdom of worship. The wise men knew they should find Jesus when he was born so they could worship him.

> **Matthew 2:1-2 (NLT)** ¹ Jesus was born in Bethlehem in Judea, during the reign of King Herod. About that time some wise men from eastern lands arrived in Jerusalem, asking, ² "Where is the newborn king of the Jews? We saw his star as it rose, and we have come to worship him."

In worship we demonstrate our love and respect to the Lord. Worship must come from our hearts. Worship prepares you for challenges and allows us to praise God in the midst of problems. Worship does something to you, in you, and for you. You have to step out from other influences to get God's directions.

> **Colossians 2:2-3 (NLT)** [2] I want them to be encouraged and knit together by strong ties of love. I want them to have complete confidence that they understand God's mysterious plan, which is Christ himself. [3] In him lie hidden all the treasures of wisdom and knowledge.

When you have a close personal relationship with God, He will bless you in ways not many people will understand. When you stay in His will, God will protect you from things that will hurt or destroy most other people.

> **Mark 16:14-18 (NLT)** [14] Still later he appeared to the eleven disciples as they were eating together. He rebuked them for their stubborn unbelief because they refused to believe those who had seen him after he had been raised from the dead. [15] And then he told them, "Go into all the world and preach the Good News to everyone. [16] Anyone who believes and is baptized will be saved. But anyone who refuses to believe will be

> condemned. [17] These miraculous signs will accompany those who believe: They will cast out demons in my name, and they will speak in new languages. [18] They will be able to handle snakes with safety, and if they drink anything poisonous, it won't hurt them. They will be able to place their hands on the sick, and they will be healed."

God will lead you to places and have you do things you never thought possible. God wants to do something today to impact tomorrow. Oftentimes, the things you do won't even be about you. God will give you the power to make a difference in the lives of others. God's doing two things in the body of the church. He has granted two different kinds of power:

1. God is increasing your power to cast out evil spirits and demons

   - You get power to live holy and overcome sin

2. Power to get wealth

When we talk about wealth, it doesn't have to mean just money. God can enable you to do things that not even money can provide. Ask God for the wisdom you need to do His will.

Empowered By Wisdom

> **Ecclesiastes 9:16-17 (NLT)** ¹⁶ So even though wisdom is better than strength, those who are wise will be despised if they are poor. What they say will not be appreciated for long. ¹⁷ Better to hear the quiet words of a wise person than the shouts of a foolish king.

You don't have to be loud and boisterous to get God's message out. You'll be off living the example of being Christ-centered than to be obnoxious in your approach to others.

> **James 5:1-4 (NLT)** ¹ Look here, you rich people: Weep and groan with anguish because of all the terrible troubles ahead of you. ² Your wealth is rotting away, and your fine clothes are moth-eaten rags. ³ Your gold and silver have become worthless. The very wealth you were counting on will eat away your flesh like fire. This treasure you have accumulated will stand as evidence against you on the day of judgment. ⁴ For listen! Hear the cries of the field workers whom you have cheated of their pay. The wages you held back cry out against you. The cries of those who harvest your fields have reached the ears of the Lord of Heaven's Armies.

Empowered By Wisdom

In the Bible, there were at least three great wealth transfers:

1. Joseph – the wealth he gained from Egypt

2. The freedom gained with people leaving Egypt

3. When Solomon gained wisdom and wealth

> **1 Kings 10:23-25 (NLT)** [23] So King Solomon became richer and wiser than any other king on earth. [24] People from every nation came to consult him and to hear the wisdom God had given him. [25] Year after year everyone who visited brought him gifts of silver and gold, clothing, weapons, spices, horses, and mules.

I know many people think money is evil. I don't think money is the problem. Like I've said before, it's the love of money that causes problems. I think God wants us to have money. I don't think he wants the love of money to control us. Did you know that God will use money to further the gospel? God will also give us money for the desires of our heart. God will use money to confirm the directions we should take. He will also use money to illustrate power.

Empowered By Wisdom

> **Proverbs 10:4 (NLT)** Lazy people are soon poor; hard workers get rich.

> **Proverbs 10:22 (NLT)** The blessing of the LORD makes a person rich, and he adds no sorrow with it.

God wants us to work for our blessings. Miracles do happen but it requires some work (our faith) for them to happen. When we consider ourselves to be "self-made" and made it to where we are in life solely due to our own efforts and nothing from God, we are subject to fail! This is not always a loss of money or status, but other problems could occur. The problem is some of us won't understand why there is a problem. If God is not behind something you own or are a part of; there will be some grief with it!

We must remind our children that in all their doing, they should seek the Lord as well. Even then it will take our children to develop their own relationship with God and seek His will. Otherwise, they may connect themselves with the wrong people.

> **Proverbs 19:14 (NLT)** Fathers can give their sons an inheritance of houses and wealth, but only the LORD can give an understanding wife.

Empowered By Wisdom

When you're in the Will of God, He will often send others to help you along the way. You must believe God can support your mission. You should become wealth-conscious. That only means you should always be looking for unexpected blessings beyond the norm. Break away from limited belief! Always remain close and faithful to God.

> **1 Samuel 2:9 (NLT)** "He will protect his faithful ones, but the wicked will disappear in darkness. No one will succeed by strength alone.

Always listen to the Word of God and be willing to gain more knowledge. In all the knowledge you gain, never let go of the fear of the Lord. I'm not talking about fear in the scary scent but in full reverence for who He is. Never try to do things your way unless you are following the Will of God.

> **Proverbs 1:29-31 (NLT)** [29] For they hated knowledge and chose not to fear the LORD. [30] They rejected my advice and paid no attention when I corrected them. [31] Therefore, they must eat the bitter fruit of living their own way, choking on their own schemes.

Quit trying to do things your way! Your way often gets things out of order. I learned several years ago you have to do first things first. When we get things out of order, chaos ensues. We sometimes try to talk our way out of our mistakes. We need to make ourselves better examples to the world. As a Christian, others should see your example and not by just your words.

> **1 Kings 5:2 - 5 (NLT)** ²Then Solomon sent this message back to Hiram: ³"You know that my father, David, was not able to build a Temple to honor the name of the LORD his God because of the many wars waged against him by surrounding nations. He could not build until the LORD gave him victory over all his enemies. ⁴But now the LORD my God has given me peace on every side; I have no enemies, and all is well. ⁵So I am planning to build a Temple to honor the name of the LORD my God, just as he had instructed my father, David. For the LORD told him, 'Your son, whom I will place on your throne, will build the Temple to honor my name.'

Solomon had a God-given purpose long before he even pursued it. God gives us a launching point and a landing point. We must handle all stages of life. A challenge is learning what you ought to be doing in each season. Going through a problem don't make you wiser, but not returning to the problem is good.

Renewal and retesting are two different things. You must know what to do at each stage so God could bless you. When it's over, it's over. There is an expression my children often hear me say, "When I'm done, I'm done!" They know that means Daddy is not going back over that problem or conversation.

God will never take you higher than your ability to get past your mistake. You got to get current affairs right before moving to the next stage. You can't be arrogant in your "David" stage. "David" stage is when you fight.

You have to deal with yourself before moving to your destiny. Solomon season is when you envision your life because you don't have to fight. Become the person God wants you to be and He will fight your battles. Become a student of the standard you want, not everyone else's standard.

> **2 Timothy 2:15 (NLT)** Work hard so you can present yourself to God and receive his approval. Be a good worker, one who does not need to be ashamed and who correctly explains the word of truth.

Empowered By Wisdom

You should strive to be one of the best workers in whatever you do. You must work in your work team and in your family as a unified body.

> **Acts 4:31 (NLT)** [31]After this prayer, the meeting place shook, and they were all filled with the Holy Spirit. Then they preached the word of God with boldness.
>
> **Acts 2:46-47 (NLT)** [46]They worshiped together at the Temple each day, met in homes for the Lord's Supper, and shared their meals with great joy and generosity — [47]all the while praising God and enjoying the goodwill of all the people. And each day the Lord added to their fellowship those who were being saved.

Unfortunately, many families and communities do not work together to improve their lives and situations. You should avoid a "crab pot" mentality. If you've ever watched a group of crabs in a pot or enclosed container, as one of them tries to get out, instead of helping each other get out, another crab will pull the one trying to get out back down. Jesus wanted us to unite and serve God together.

> **John 17:11 (NLT)** [11]Now I am departing from the world; they are staying in this

> world, but I am coming to you. Holy Father, you have given me your name; now protect them by the power of your name so that they will be united just as we are.

There are five things we need to be "one" in:

1. One heart

2. Giving

> **Romans 15:5 - 6 (NLT)** ⁵May God, who gives this patience and encouragement, help you live in complete harmony with each other, as is fitting for followers of Christ Jesus. ⁶Then all of you can join together with one voice, giving praise and glory to God, the Father of our Lord Jesus Christ.

3. One mind

4. One voice

> **Habakkuk 2:2-3 (NLT)** ² Then the LORD said to me, "Write my answer

plainly on tablets, so that a runner can carry the correct message to others. [3] This vision is for a future time. It describes the end, and it will be fulfilled. If it seems slow in coming, wait patiently, for it will surely take place. It will not be delayed.

When God's words go out it will not return void

5. One love

The Bible said that wisdom shouts in the streets:

Proverbs 1:20-23 (NLT) [20] Wisdom shouts in the streets. She cries out in the public square. [21] She calls to the crowds along the main street, to those gathered in front of the city gate: [22] "How long, you simpletons, will you insist on being simpleminded? How long will you mockers relish your mocking? How long will you fools hate knowledge? [23] Come and listen to my counsel. I'll share my heart with you and make you wise.

Wisdom is having faith that God will give you your portion. If God told you something, He will do it!

> **Ezekiel 36:33 - 36 (NLT)** ³³"This is what the Sovereign LORD says: When I cleanse you from your sins, I will repopulate your cities, and the ruins will be rebuilt. ³⁴The fields that used to lie empty and desolate in plain view of everyone will again be farmed. ³⁵And when I bring you back, people will say, 'This former wasteland is now like the Garden of Eden! The abandoned and ruined cities now have strong walls and are filled with people!' ³⁶Then the surrounding nations that survive will know that I, the LORD, have rebuilt the ruins and replanted the wasteland. For I, the LORD, have spoken, and I will do what I say.

Don't be discouraged by your situation. When God does certain things for you, it's not always about you. God will bless you despite of you. There are some things you can only get from God. When God delivers you from something, give God the glory. God said he would sprinkle us with clean water. Whatever your situation, God can fix it!

> **1 Corinthians 1:30-31 (NLT)** ³⁰God has united you with Christ Jesus. For our benefit God made him to be wisdom itself. Christ made us right with God; he made us pure and holy, and he freed us

from sin. ³¹Therefore, as the Scriptures say, "If you want to boast, boast only about the LORD."

When we change our minds, God will deliver us from our snares. That's right, sometimes we set our snares for others to fall into, only to get caught in our own trap. God can also deliver us from the snares others set for us.

> **Psalms 91:1-6 (NLT)** ¹ Those who live in the shelter of the Most High will find rest in the shadow of the Almighty. ² This I declare about the LORD: He alone is my refuge, my place of safety; he is my God, and I trust him. ³ For he will rescue you from every trap and protect you from deadly disease. ⁴ He will cover you with his feathers. He will shelter you with his wings. His faithful promises are your armor and protection. ⁵ Do not be afraid of the terrors of the night, nor the arrow that flies in the day. ⁶ Do not dread the disease that stalks in darkness, nor the disaster that strikes at midday.

The enemy is real! The enemy wants to annihilate us. We're in spiritual warfare. You must know that no man can serve two masters. We must put God first in our lives.

We must be obedient to God's words and put faith into action.

> **1 Timothy 6:20-21 (NLT)** [20]Timothy, guard what God has entrusted to you. Avoid godless, foolish discussions with those who oppose you with their so-called knowledge. [21]Some people have wandered from the faith by following such foolishness. May God's grace be with you all.

In our time for change, we should try to change the world and not let the world change us. We should try to change our lives for the better and make a difference in the lives of others.

> **Numbers 13:30 - 31 (NLT)** [30]But Caleb tried to quiet the people as they stood before Moses. "Let's go at once to take the land," he said. "We can certainly conquer it!" [31]But the other men who had explored the land with him disagreed. "We can't go up against them! They are stronger than we are!"

We need to change our words! How can you get ready to do battle if you are saying you can't win before the battle begins?

Change is obvious when progress is made. Change is demanded as we move forward. The devil keeps us quiet when we should be talking. When you speak, speak words of construction, not destruction.

> **Genesis 1:26 (NLT)** ²⁶Then God said, "Let us make human beings in our image, to be like ourselves. They will reign over the fish in the sea, the birds in the sky, the livestock, all the wild animals on the earth, and the small animals that scurry along the ground."

Since God placed mankind in charge, we as believers need to say what life is going to be. Take dominion over your words – there is power in words.

Proverbs 18:21 says your words are powerful!

> **Proverbs 18:20 - 21 (NLT)** ²⁰ Wise words satisfy like a good meal; the right words bring satisfaction. ²¹ The tongue can bring death or life; those who love to talk will reap the consequences.

Jesus spoke out against bad things that comes out of people's mouths.

> **Matthew 15:11 (NLT)** ¹¹It's not what goes into your mouth that defiles you; you are defiled by the words that come out of your mouth."

Use your words to uplift your situation or the situations of others. You need to speak positively over your life if you want to go to place of more than enough. The challenge of changing your words is necessary.

Your words are a contract, but unlike a contract, they are not retractable. You've experienced your saying something bad to someone only to wish you could take your words back. Too late, the damage is done. However, through God's mercy, you can change your words to words of comfort.

> **Mark 11:22 - 24 (NLT)** ²²Then Jesus said to the disciples, "Have faith in God. ²³I tell you the truth, you can say to this mountain, 'May you be lifted up and thrown into the sea,' and it will happen. But you must really believe it will happen and have no doubt in your heart. ²⁴I tell you, you can pray for anything,

> and if you believe that you've received it, it will be yours.

Change what you order in life to change the outcome. When you have faith that God will deliver you from something, say it out loud with confidence!

Romans 10:17 says faith comes from hearing, that is, hearing the Good News about Christ. Not only do you have to hear the Word of God, you have to put things in action. Guard your mind and talk faith. Romans 10:8 says, "The message is very close at hand; it is on your lips and in our heart."

> **Mark 5:35 - 36 (NLT)** ³⁵While he was still speaking to her, messengers arrived from the home of Jairus, the leader of the synagogue. They told him, "Your daughter is dead. There's no use troubling the Teacher now." ³⁶But Jesus overheard them and said to Jairus, "Don't be afraid. Just have faith."

God will do things in your life that no one else understands how it happened. The same people who were once against you will do something that helps you.

> **Romans 8:31 (NLT)** ³¹What shall we say about such wonderful things as these? If God is for us, who can ever be against us?

Your response to difficulty will determine how you come out of it. When something bad happens to you, you can't fall apart. Pray about it and let God take care of the problem. Sometimes His way of taking care of the problem might be in His telling you how to handle the problem.

It's time to make a change and realize you are not in total control of your life. Your first change has to be an internal change. Your attitude is a part of this change. Your attitude determines your altitude. You have to change your personal, family, and church life. Don't pass along bad family traditions. Choose to change these traditions.

To change you must be willing to take risks. Old friends might want to keep you where you are. They don't always do it on purpose. It's just easier for them to keep you where they are in life.

There are three types of people:

- Changeable - People who hear the Word of God, and are willing to change.
- Unchangeable - People who are unwilling to change, no matter the information they receive.
- People Who Cause Change – they do things to make you want to change.

In your church life, the challenge is to move away from being just a church member or an attender to a solid Christian! You need to be more in your church than someone that just shows up on Sundays.

You have to make a personal choice to change. You should have a desire to be exceptional. Solid people develop solid families, solid families develop solid churches. Don't be fair weather Christians.

> **Ecclesiastes 9:17 (NLT)** [17] Better to hear the quiet words of a wise person than the shouts of a foolish king.

Some folk come into your life for a season, others for a reason. Don't make such a big fuss when one of these people decide to walk out of your life. Wish them well and press on with your life.

> **Luke 6:47-49 (NLT)** [47] I will show you what it's like when someone comes to me, listens to my teaching, and then follows it. [48] It is like a person building a house who digs deep and lays the foundation on solid rock. When the floodwaters rise and break against the house, it stands firm because it is well built. [49] But anyone who hears and doesn't obey is like a person who builds a

house without a foundation. When the floods sweep down against that house, it will collapse into a heap of ruins."

A solid life is built on the Word of God. Anything else if just folly and subject to fail in some way.

> **Ephesians 1:16-17 (NLT)** [16]I have not stopped thanking God for you. I pray for you constantly, [17] asking God, the glorious Father of our Lord Jesus Christ, to give you spiritual wisdom and insight so that you might grow in your knowledge of God.

As I said before, wisdom and knowledge are two different things. You can gain knowledge through education and life's experiences but you have wisdom when you are able to successfully use that knowledge in a positive direction.

> **Ecclesiastes 12:9-12 (NLT)** [9]Keep this in mind: The Teacher was considered wise, and he taught the people everything he knew. He listened carefully to many proverbs, studying and classifying them. [10]The Teacher sought to find just the right words to express truths clearly. [11]The words of the wise are like cattle

> prods—painful but helpful. Their collected sayings are like a nail-studded stick with which a shepherd drives the sheep. ¹²But, my child, let me give you some further advice: Be careful, for writing books is endless, and much study wears you out.

My gift is writing and I only do so when God inspires me. Your actions should have a balance between what you have to do and what you desire to do. You have to balance your personal life with that of family and a job or business.

> **Deuteronomy 11:13-15 (NLT)** ¹³ "If you carefully obey all the commands I am giving you today, and if you love the LORD your God and serve him with all your heart and soul, ¹⁴ then he will send the rains in their proper seasons—the early and late rains—so you can bring in your harvests of grain, new wine, and olive oil. ¹⁵ He will give you lush pastureland for your livestock, and you yourselves will have all you want to eat.

You can't always stay where you are to get to where God wants you to be. You have to get ready for the journey. This journey does not always have to be a physical journey. A spiritual journey may be what's needed.

> **Leviticus 25:18 (NLT)** 18"If you want to live securely in the land, follow my decrees and obey my regulations.

When you get to where God wants you to be at a certain point in time (it changes for some people), you have to continue listening to God's instructions. Nothing can stop God's blessings. These can include debt reduction, and debt cancellation. You need to ask God to come against any season of lack. Then you need to walk past people's opinions of you. Even when you are doing well, some people will still think negatively of you.

> **Psalms 1:1-2 (NLT)** 1 Oh, the joys of those who do not follow the advice of the wicked, or stand around with sinners, or join in with mockers. 2 But they delight in the law of the LORD, meditating on it day and night.

When you follow the Word of God, the wisdom you gain will help you face the future confidently. Don't hesitant when God directs you to do something.

> **James 4:14-17 (NLT)** 14 How do you know what your life will be like

> tomorrow? Your life is like the morning fog—it's here a little while, then it's gone. ¹⁵ What you ought to say is, "If the Lord wants us to, we will live and do this or that." ¹⁶Otherwise you are boasting about your own plans, and all such boasting is evil. ¹⁷ Remember, it is sin to know what you ought to do and then not do it.

Some of you have to plan for everything you do in life. There is nothing wrong with that so long as you realize you are not totally in control of things that happen to you. I will say again, you do what you can and let God do the rest. However, if God tells you to stand still or keep quiet, do so.

> **Proverbs 16:9 (NLT)** ⁹ We can make our plans, but the LORD determines our steps.

There are three things to avoid:

1. Planning without God

2. Worrying about tomorrow

3. Putting off doing what's right

Empowered By Wisdom

1 John 2:14 says, God's word lives in your hearts, and you have won your battle with the evil one. This means you are victorious even before the battle begins.

Don't Be Deceived

Whatever you do, don't let your wisdom and knowledge mislead you.

> **Isaiah 47:10-11 (NLT)** [10] "You felt secure in your wickedness. 'No one sees me,' you said. But your 'wisdom' and 'knowledge' have led you astray, and you said, 'I am the only one, and there is no other.' [11] So disaster will overtake you, and you won't be able to charm it away. Calamity will fall upon you, and you won't be able to buy your way out. A catastrophe will strike you suddenly, one for which you are not prepared.

"Wisdom without courage leaves an empty space that time will soon betray" - Ron Miller. As mentioned before, you need to have courage to act in faith. This courage, enhanced by wisdom, will propel you into a great future!

> **Colossians 2:1-5 (NLT)** [1] I want you to know how much I have agonized for you and for the church at Laodicea, and for many other believers who have never met me personally. [2] I want them to be encouraged and knit together by strong

> ties of love. I want them to have complete confidence that they understand God's mysterious plan, which is Christ himself. ³In him lie hidden all the treasures of wisdom and knowledge. ⁴I am telling you this so no one will deceive you with well-crafted arguments. ⁵For though I am far away from you, my heart is with you. And I rejoice that you are living as you should and that your faith in Christ is strong.

You should use your knowledge while growing in faith. The knowledge you gain will help you gain the wisdom to make wise decisions. God has already equipped you with an ability to gain knowledge to build upon the wisdom you need for a successful life and to reach your short and long term goals. Once again, you have to pray for and seek Godly wisdom.

> **2 Peter 1:3-4 (NLT)** ³By his divine power, God has given us everything we need for living a godly life. We have received all of this by coming to know him, the one who called us to himself by means of his marvelous glory and excellence. ⁴And because of his glory and excellence, he has given us great and precious promises. These are the promises that enable you to share his

divine nature and escape the world's corruption caused by human desires.

Some of us men desire to be with the woman of our dreams. Unfortunately, we date and seek women for the wrong reasons. We get entangled with a woman we didn't pray about and then wonder why God is punishing us with our mate's actions. In many cases, we chose that woman and didn't wait for God to give us the right one. There is a special occasion when God gives us a good woman. There are certain things that happen when a man loves a woman.

> **Genesis 2:18 - 22 (NLT)** [18]Then the LORD God said, "It is not good for the man to be alone. I will make a helper who is just right for him." [19]So the LORD God formed from the ground all the wild animals and all the birds of the sky. He brought them to the man to see what he would call them, and the man chose a name for each one. [20]He gave names to all the livestock, all the birds of the sky, and all the wild animals. But still there was no helper just right for him. [21]So the LORD God caused the man to fall into a deep sleep. While the man slept, the LORD God took out one of the man's ribs and closed up the opening. [22]Then the LORD God made a woman from the rib, and he brought her to the man.

Whether or not you're with the right person or not, relationships require a lot of work. There are two reasons some relationships don't work. 1) You're with the right person, but loving them the wrong way. You neglect the relationship by not listening to your spouse, not spending time with her, etc. 2) You're married to the wrong person, but still love them the right way. In this case, you can't give enough of what she needs.

Women want you to love them as an individual. Be specific when you compliment them. These are the things a woman wants:

- wants to be your top priority
- wants to know she's closest to you
- wants you to brag on her to family
- wants you to think she's beautiful

If you've made mistakes in your relationship, apologize and look for ways to make it better.

> **2 Peter 1:5-9 (NLT)** ⁵In view of all this, make every effort to respond to God's promises. Supplement your faith with a generous provision of moral excellence, and moral excellence with knowledge, ⁶and knowledge with self-control, and self-control with patient endurance, and patient endurance with godliness, ⁷and godliness with brotherly affection, and brotherly affection with

> love for everyone. ⁸The more you grow like this, the more productive and useful you will be in your knowledge of our Lord Jesus Christ. ⁹But those who fail to develop in this way are shortsighted or blind, forgetting that they have been cleansed from their old sins.

One problem I see, especially among women, is when we place a person above all else in life. You should never place anyone or anything before God. Let nothing move you from your place with God.

> **1 Corinthians 15:56-58 (NLT)** ⁵⁶For sin is the sting that results in death, and the law gives sin its power. ⁵⁷But thank God! He gives us victory over sin and death through our Lord Jesus Christ. ⁵⁸So, my dear brothers and sisters, be strong and immovable. Always work enthusiastically for the Lord, for you know that nothing you do for the Lord is ever useless.

Be humble in your approach to announcing your accomplishments in life. Even if you don't acknowledge God enabling you to get where you are, He was there. Watch out, for some of us educated folks think we know everything!

> **1 Corinthians 8:2-3 (NLT)** ²Anyone who claims to know all the answers doesn't really know very much. ³But the person who loves God is the one whom God recognizes.

Through all you do, always trust the Lord! You are special but it doesn't mean you have to put someone else down to show who you are. Call on the Lord when you need help, not man. (Note: Sometimes God sends a person to help you)

> **Psalms 4:3 (NLT)** ³ You can be sure of this: The LORD set apart the godly for himself. The LORD will answer when I call to him.

You might give credit to where you are and place your security in your political influence, job connections, status, rank, or even your college fraternity or sorority but this should not be so. Don't put your security into anything but the Lord.

> **1 Peter 4:1-2 (NLT)** ¹So then, since Christ suffered physical pain, you must arm yourselves with the same attitude he

had, and be ready to suffer, too. For if you have suffered physically for Christ, you have finished with sin. ²You won't spend the rest of your lives chasing your own desires, but you will be anxious to do the will of God.

Ask God what His will is for your life. Do His will no matter how crazy it may sound. Even Moses questioned God when God told Moses to deliver his people from Egypt.

Exodus 3:9 - 12 (NLT) ⁹Look! The cry of the people of Israel has reached me, and I have seen how harshly the Egyptians abuse them. ¹⁰Now go, for I am sending you to Pharaoh. You must lead my people Israel out of Egypt." ¹¹But Moses protested to God, "Who am I to appear before Pharaoh? Who am I to lead the people of Israel out of Egypt?" ¹²God answered, "I will be with you. And this is your sign that I am the one who has sent you: When you have brought the people out of Egypt, you will worship God at this very mountain."

Let God continue to work on you. We are constantly under construction in our lives. God will work on you but you have work to do yourself. God uses people who are industrious and not those who are lazy. While you're doing what God will have you do you must understand that you may not understand everything God's wants you to do. Let go of the importance of needing to understand.

In the Bible, God tells his children who they are. "I am" tells me who I am. Don't let anybody else tell you who you are. While you're under construction, don't establish friendship with someone with mutual dislikes. This just slows you down and makes you less willing to change. When God is finished, you'll be like gold.

> **1 Samuel 17:23 - 24 (NLT)** 23As he was talking with them, Goliath, the Philistine champion from Gath, came out from the Philistine ranks. Then David heard him shout his usual taunt to the army of Israel. 24As soon as the Israelite army saw him, they began to run away in fright.

David had a very large and frightful enemy to face. The bigger your enemy, the bigger the blessing. You have to say to yourself, "I will believe that I will get what I need". As I said before, not only will God provide for you, he will fight your battles as well.

> **Jeremiah 1:18-19 (NLT)** ¹⁸ For see, today I have made you strong like a fortified city that cannot be captured, like an iron pillar or a bronze wall. You will stand against the whole land — the kings, officials, priests, and people of Judah. ¹⁹ They will fight you, but they will fail. For I am with you, and I will take care of you. I, the LORD, have spoken!"

God is your creator! There is no one greater than Him. You should never question what God is able to do for you.

> **Isaiah 29:16 (NLT)** ¹⁶ How foolish can you be? He is the Potter, and he is certainly greater than you, the clay! Should the created thing say of the one who made it, "He didn't make me"? Does a jar ever say, "The potter who made me is stupid"?

Ask God about the things you want and need in your life. Keep in mind whatever you want, wants you. So you have to really be careful about the things you ask God for or the things you never asked God about but want them anyway. Sometimes we have to go through something to get something we want or to a place we want to be. You know that God is in your life when you go through something and you survive it.

More than often I have said God has things in store for you in your life. However, you might miss your blessings if you are not wise enough to pay attention to God's instructions. You're destined for greatness! God will bless you even if the odds are against you. The story of Gideon fighting against the Midianites is just one example. Gideon had over from 30,000 men ready to fight the battle against the Midianites. God told Gideon to reduce the size of his Army. By man's knowledge and standards, Gideon needed his entire army to fight the planned battle. He eventually ended up with 300 men.

> **Judges 7:7 - 8 (NLT)** [7]The LORD told Gideon, "With these 300 men I will rescue you and give you victory over the Midianites. Send all the others home." [8]So Gideon collected the provisions and rams' horns of the other warriors and sent them home. But he kept the 300 men with him. The Midianite camp was in the valley just below Gideon.

When He delivers you, God wants all the glory! Your victory isn't decided by friends or family, it's decided by faith. Fear and faith cannot operate at the same time. You have to loose dead weight; as Gideon did when he reduced the size of his army. You have to trust God with your whole heart.

> **Judges 7:4 - 5 (NLT)** ⁴But the LORD told Gideon, "There are still too many! Bring them down to the spring, and I will test them to determine who will go with you and who will not." ⁵When Gideon took his warriors down to the water, the LORD told him, "Divide the men into two groups. In one group put all those who cup water in their hands and lap it up with their tongues like dogs. In the other group put all those who kneel down and drink with their mouths in the stream."

In this case God was showing Gideon (and us) that a few will do. You don't always need what the world tells you when God has placed a mission in your hearts. Even if you say you only have a little, God can use what you got.

Empowered By Wisdom

Ask God For Wisdom

In the Bible, James 1:5 says for us to ask for wisdom.

> **James 1:5 (NLT)** [5]If you need wisdom, ask our generous God, and he will give it to you. He will not rebuke you for asking.

Solomon asked God for wisdom. Wisdom is something we should seek from God daily. It pleases God that we ask him for wisdom versus us relying upon our own wisdom, or the lack thereof.

> **1 Kings 3:10-14 (NLT)** [10]The Lord was pleased that Solomon had asked for wisdom. [11]So God replied, "Because you have asked for wisdom in governing my people with justice and have not asked for a long life or wealth or the death of your enemies— [12]I will give you what you asked for! I will give you a wise and understanding heart such as no one else has had or ever will have! [13]And I will also give you what you did not ask for— riches and fame! No other king in all the world will be compared to you for the rest of your life! [14]And if you follow me and obey my decrees and my commands

Empowered By Wisdom

<blockquote>as your father, David, did, I will give you a long life."</blockquote>

Your life can be just as phenomenal! When will you realize that with Godly wisdom you can do anything positive you set your mind to!

The story of King Solomon's judgment based on wisdom is told in 1 Kings 3:16 – 28. Two prostitutes came to Solomon to solve a problem they were having. One woman said she and the other woman lived in one house; and she and the other woman both delivered a child in the house. The other woman delivered her baby three days after the first woman and there was no one else in the house but the two of them and their babies. The first woman claimed the other woman's child died in the night because she laid on it. The first woman claimed the second woman arose at midnight and then took the first lady's son from beside her and laid the baby at the second woman's bosom. The second lady then laid her dead child at the first woman's bosom. The first woman said when she awoke in the morning to nurse her child, it was dead. The woman then said when she had a chance to consider things later that morning, she realized the dead baby was not the son she bore.

The other woman said, no, the living was her son, and the dead one was the first woman's son. The women argued before King Solomon and the first woman said, no, the dead child belonged to the second woman, and the living child was her son.

Then Solomon spoke out and said one of you is saying the living child is yours and the dead one belongs to the other woman while the other woman is saying the living child is hers. And the king said to bring him a sword. And they brought King Solomon a sword.

And King Solomon said, divide the living child in two, and give half to the first woman, and half to the other woman. Then the second woman, who really was the child's mother, said, O my lord, give her the living child, and in no way slay it. But the other said, Let it be neither mine nor thine, but divide it. Then the king answered and said to give the second woman the living child, for Solomon had the wisdom to know that a loving mother would not let harm come to her child.

> **1 Kings 3:28 (NLT)** [28]When all Israel heard the king's decision, the people were in awe of the king, for they saw the wisdom God had given him for rendering justice.

Solomon was not the first man that realized he needed Godly wisdom to live a successful live. King David, Solomon's father, told Solomon he should seek Godly wisdom, as he did.

Empowered By Wisdom

> **1 Chronicles 22:11-13 (NLT)** [11]"Now, my son, may the LORD be with you and give you success as you follow his directions in building the Temple of the LORD your God. [12]And may the LORD give you wisdom and understanding, that you may obey the Law of the LORD your God as you rule over Israel. [13]For you will be successful if you carefully obey the decrees and regulations that the LORD gave to Israel through Moses. Be strong and courageous; do not be afraid or lose heart!

Solomon, in his desire to follow the Lord as his father David did, asked God early on for wisdom. Solomon was aware of the source of his father's success in leadership and wanted the same for his own leadership.

> **2 Chronicles 1:8-10 (NLT)** [8]Solomon replied to God, "You showed faithful love to David, my father, and now you have made me king in his place. [9]O LORD God, please continue to keep your promise to David my father, for you have made me king over a people as numerous as the dust of the earth! [10]Give me the wisdom and knowledge to lead them properly, for who could possibly govern this great people of yours?"

Jesus was anointed. He was sent down in bodily form so that people who had not seen God would be able to associate his presence with that of God's. In the same sense, your body is not you. You are inside (spiritual). Your body is a carrier of your spirit. So take care of the temple God blessed you to be but remember your spirit is more important. We gain wisdom as we endure the physical realm our bodies are a part of.

> **Psalms 90:9-12 (NLT)** ⁹ We live our lives beneath your wrath, ending our years with a groan. ¹⁰ Seventy years are given to us! Some even live to eighty. But even the best years are filled with pain and trouble; soon they disappear, and we fly away. ¹¹ Who can comprehend the power of your anger? Your wrath is as awesome as the fear you deserve. ¹² Teach us to realize the brevity of life, so that we may grow in wisdom.

With that said, we need to make every day count. I suggest you take inventory of your blessings. Then you will realize that regardless of your situation, God has blessed you in so many other ways. You may be able to avoid many things but there will be some suffering from being a Christian.

Empowered By Wisdom

> **1 Peter 4:12-17 (NLT)** [12] Dear friends, don't be surprised at the fiery trials you are going through, as if something strange were happening to you. [13] Instead, be very glad—for these trials make you partners with Christ in his suffering, so that you will have the wonderful joy of seeing his glory when it is revealed to all the world. [14] So be happy when you are insulted for being a Christian, for then the glorious Spirit of God rests upon you. [15] If you suffer, however, it must not be for murder, stealing, making trouble, or prying into other people's affairs. [16] But it is no shame to suffer for being a Christian. Praise God for the privilege of being called by his name! [17] For the time has come for judgment, and it must begin with God's household. And if judgment begins with us, what terrible fate awaits those who have never obeyed God's Good News?

So you can stop asking that question I used to ask so much, "Lord, why me?" Now you should realize, "Why not me?" Just keep in praising the Lord and he shall deliver you.

> **Psalms 42:11 (NLT)** [11] Why am I discouraged? Why is my heart so sad? I

Empowered By Wisdom

> will put my hope in God! I will praise him again — my Savior and my God!

We must learn how to stand under pressure! Let's face it, we all have problems. We can't give up because the pressure is too high. We must seek God's help in dealing with life's problems.

> **Daniel 2:18-21 (NLT)** [18] He urged them to ask the God of heaven to show them his mercy by telling them the secret, so they would not be executed along with the other wise men of Babylon. [19] That night the secret was revealed to Daniel in a vision. Then Daniel praised the God of heaven. [20] He said, "Praise the name of God forever and ever, for he has all wisdom and power. [21] He controls the course of world events; he removes kings and sets up other kings. He gives wisdom to the wise and knowledge to the scholars.

God can give you direction in dreams. When we see things in a dream we wonder why we dreamt it and when will it happen. We get impatient and wonder, are we there yet? We should ask God if we're on the right track in our lives. We develop our own opinions on how things should go and where we should be. We don't like changing our minds about things we thought we were sure of. Allow God to show you what is right.

> **Acts 10:15 (NLT)** ¹⁵But the voice spoke again: "Do not call something unclean if God has made it clean."

Sometimes when God allows bad things to happen, innocent people will sometimes get hurt. That's why it's important to listen to that inner voice that tells you not to go a certain way when you driving or not to go to a certain place you previously wanted to go. No matter what, stay on God's good side and you will survive the bad things that happened when you just happen to be in the wrong place at the time.

> **Acts 10:34-35 (NLT)** ³⁴ Then Peter replied, "I see very clearly that God shows no favoritism. ³⁵In every nation he accepts those who fear him and do what is right.

James 1:5 said we should ask for wisdom. Wisdom will enable us to make the right decisions about our daily lives. It will tell us not to go to a certain place where we know we shouldn't. It will cause us to make the right decisions about our personal and professional affairs.

> **James 1:5 - 6 (NLT)** ⁵If you need wisdom, ask our generous God, and he will give it to you. He will not rebuke you for asking. ⁶But when you ask him, be sure that your faith is in God alone. Do not waver, for a person with divided loyalty is as unsettled as a wave of the sea that is blown and tossed by the wind.

If you're looking for a mate, you should go to God first. I know you think this is too mundane, but it's the right way to go. We all too often have our personal preferences in the persons we think we should be attracted to. There is nothing wrong with preferences but they are more often based on lustful foundations than they are character focused. If you want a match made in heaven, then ask God for it!

> **Genesis 2:18 (NLT)** ¹⁸Then the LORD God said, "It is not good for the man to be alone. I will make a helper who is just right for him."

Most importantly, we must ask God first to give us a companion that will be good to us. God wants you to have joy, not just be happy. Joy is a continuous thing whereas happiness fluctuates depending on how things are going. Marriages lasts longer if made by heaven. A man has to die to his flesh and have a new beginning with his wife.

Empowered By Wisdom

> **Genesis 2:24 (NLT)** 24This explains why a man leaves his father and mother and is joined to his wife, and the two are united into one.

When God makes it right for us, we fear it for it seems too hard to believe. Sometimes we have to just do it! God is waiting for us to act on something he asked us to do. God has more in store for our lives. Sometimes when God shows up, we don't recognize it. If you call on Jesus, He will show up. Matthew 14:26 says don't be afraid.

> **Matthew 14:27 (NLT)** 27But Jesus spoke to them at once. "Don't be afraid," he said. "Take courage. I am here!"

You, too, should ask God for wisdom - not just common wisdom but godly wisdom! This is the only type of wisdom that is enduring. Godly wisdom is unfailing and sure to get you the right results!

Empowered By Wisdom

Wisdom Gives You Better Vision

Do you have 20/20 vision? The American Optometric Association (AOA) defines 20/20 vision as a term used to express normal visual acuity (the clarity or sharpness of vision) measured at a distance of 20 feet. (The American Optometric Association (AOA), 2014) If you have 20/20 vision, you can see clearly at 20 feet what should normally be seen at that distance. If you have 20/100 vision, it means that you must be as close as 20 feet to see what a person with normal vision can see at 100 feet. Having 20/20 vision does not necessarily mean perfect vision. To have 20/20 vision only indicates the sharpness or clarity of vision at a distance.

Some people can see well at a distance, but are unable to bring nearer objects into focus. This condition can be caused by farsightedness or a loss of focusing ability. Others can see items that are close, but cannot see those far away (nearsightedness). A comprehensive eye examination by a doctor of optometry can diagnose those causes, if any, that are affecting your ability to see well. In most cases, your optometrist can prescribe glasses, contact lenses or a vision therapy program that will help improve your vision.

This is all based on the physical vision. What I am talking about now is spiritual vision. What you allow to come into your body in the physical sense can have an effect on your spiritual vision. This is why Christians should avoid watching any pornography and limit morally decrepit media content on TV, movies, books, and the Internet.

> **Matthew 6:22-24 (NLT)** [22]"Your eye is a lamp that provides light for your body. When your eye is good, your whole body is filled with light. [23]But when your eye is bad, your whole body is filled with darkness. And if the light you think you have is actually darkness, how deep that darkness is! [24]"No one can serve two masters. For you will hate one and love the other; you will be devoted to one and despise the other. You cannot serve both God and money.

How many times have you prayed for something and become disappointed because what you prayed for didn't come or happen? Some people will tell you that prayer is a waste of time and things that occur afterwards is just happenchance. Let me tell you that prayer is real and God hears you. When you pray for something, how bad do you want it?

> **Luke 11:9-10 (NLT)** [9]"And so I tell you, keep on asking, and you will receive what you ask for. Keep on seeking, and you will find. Keep on knocking, and the

door will be opened to you. ¹⁰ For everyone who asks, receives. Everyone who seeks, finds. And to everyone who knocks, the door will be opened.

There are three answers to prayer

1. Yes, what you want is good and God wants it for you.
2. No, what you're praying for is not for you.
3. Wait, it's not time. One of the hardest answers we will get is wait. Sometimes we just don't get the message. When we do, we ask, "Lord, how long must I?

The truth is, God has something designed just for you. So waiting sometimes has an unseen purpose.

> **James 4:2-3 (NLT)** ²You want what you don't have, so you scheme and kill to get it. You are jealous of what others have, but you can't get it, so you fight and wage war to take it away from them. Yet you don't have what you want because you don't ask God for it. ³And even when you ask, you don't get it because your motives are all wrong—you want only what will give you pleasure.

Some of us give up too soon with what we ask God for. If it doesn't happen when we expected it, we have a tendency to try to do it ourselves and mess things up. How many times have you bought things only to later wish you never had or got involved in something only to realize it was a mistake? That was because we either didn't ask God, didn't wait on God, or didn't like His answer and decided to move forward anyway.

Even if we are sure we are on the right track we get pushback sometimes and wonder why we can't get the thing done. We should go to God with things that only He can do.
Asking is being verbal, seeking is being visual and looking for results. Wherever God gives vision, He provides provision. You can always count him to provide if He meant something for you. You must keep the faith. The devil will mess with you to keep you from having faith. Sometimes you have to snatch your blessings out of the devil's hands!

> **Hebrews 11:6 (NLT)** ⁶And it is impossible to please God without faith. Anyone who wants to come to him must believe that God exists and that he rewards those who sincerely seek him.

You and God

One question I would like to ask you is, what are you looking for in life? Another is what are you expecting from your current situation? The Bible says you should cast all your cares unto The Lord. The Lord has all the answers to your questions if you just heed His Word and His will. God will bless you with all the knowledge you need to make wise decisions. Sight is very important in gaining knowledge. If you want 20/20 vision, you have to get check-ups. In the physical sense, you can see an optometrist. In the spiritual sense, you need to seek out the vision God wants you to have.

> **Genesis 3:1-7 (NLT)** [1]The serpent was the shrewdest of all the wild animals the LORD God had made. One day he asked the woman, "Did God really say you must not eat the fruit from any of the trees in the garden?" [2]"Of course we may eat fruit from the trees in the garden," the woman replied. [3]"It's only the fruit from the tree in the middle of the garden that we are not allowed to eat. God said, 'You must not eat it or even touch it; if you do, you will die.'" [4]"You won't die!" the serpent replied to the woman. [5]"God knows that your eyes will be opened as soon as you eat it, and you will be like God, knowing both good and evil." [6]The woman was convinced. She saw that the

> tree was beautiful and its fruit looked delicious, and she wanted the wisdom it would give her. So she took some of the fruit and ate it. Then she gave some to her husband, who was with her, and he ate it, too. ⁷At that moment their eyes were opened, and they suddenly felt shame at their nakedness. So they sewed <u>fig leaves together to cover themselves.</u>

The problem was Adam and Eve were deceived by what they saw. It wasn't so much the fact that they saw the fig tree. The problem was due to the fact they were told not to partake of the fruit of the tree. The serpent convinced Eve that regardless of what God told Adam, eating the fruit will be rewarding. I believe Adam and Eve both had good physical sight; however, were limited in spiritual sight and obedience.

The physical condition of your eye determines the amount and quality of light that comes in. This also applies to spiritual condition. There are four questions I will ask you.

1. How do you see God?

I know you've heard the expression that God is love. I think this is the undeniable truth. God loves us so much that he gave his only begotten son. How many of you are willing to make the same sacrifice? One of God's commandments was that we love one another. You can hate mankind and then say you love God. The Bible tells us that God made us in his own image. Learn how to love people.

> **1 John 4:7-8 (NLT)** Dear friends, let us continue to love one another, for love comes from God. Anyone who loves is a child of God and knows God. But anyone who does not love does not know God, for God is love.

2. How do you see Jesus?

Jesus was sent down in the flesh so we could understand God and the Holy Spirit in the spiritual realm. You must be wise and faithful enough to believe that God is real and Jesus is our Lord and Savior.

> **2 Peter 3:17-18 (NLT)** [17]I am warning you ahead of time, dear friends. Be on guard so that you will not be carried away by the errors of these wicked people and lose your own secure footing. [18]Rather, you must grow in the grace and knowledge of our Lord and Savior Jesus Christ. All glory to him, both now and forever! Amen.

3. How do you see your situation? Sometimes your outlook to your problem will affect the outcome. How can you see your way out of something when you feel so hopeless that when the opportune moment or the solution appears you don't even reach for it since you don't expect things to ever change? Don't look at your bad situation as being permanent. God can bless you through any of your circumstances. I hope you take a moment and learn something from your experience.

4. How do you see yourself? I have some very beautiful people on the outside but if you only got to know them closely you'd realize they don't think much of themselves. The funny thing about external beauty is that if you are not statistically beautiful (beauty defined by mankind and that of society), but if you think of yourself as being beautiful, it will radiate and someone is bound to notice that beauty. We people sometimes focus too much on physical beauty. If you think of yourself as a child of God, then you will carry yourself as a child of royalty. That internal beauty cannot be denied. You'll feel better about yourself and won't let anything keep you down for long. Reach out to God and let him know how you're feeling. Seek the joy of the Lord and find your spirit being lifted out of self-doubt and pity!

Check your appearance to see your short-comings. We all have faults and we all have our individual issue. None of us are perfect. Recognizing your issues should give you a chance to ask God to work on you. You should never see your shortcoming and weaknesses as your identity that you can't escape.

God wants us all to come as we are. It does not mean we should stay as we are! Personalities don't always have to change for God can use you as you are; however, bad habits and inappropriate behaviors and practices need to be changed. Again, it's time for a change for the better.

First, it's time to avoid fatal distractions. Distractions will take your focus away from the good things God intends for you to do. This may be something as simple of partying more than you're studying while you're in college. The distraction is the keep you from being as good at your course of study as God intended you to be. Other distractions can be people such as unbelieving family members, jealous friends, or even a boyfriend, girlfriend, or a spouse. If it's your spouse, you should continue to love them but it does not mean you should allow them to distract you from your purpose, especially if God clearly showed you what He wants you to do. Also avoid false teachings and sneaky people.

> **Galatians 5:7-10 (NLT)** 7You were running the race so well. Who has held you back from following the truth? 8It certainly isn't God, for he is the one who called you to freedom. 9This false teaching is like a little yeast that spreads through the whole batch of dough! 10I am trusting the Lord to keep you from believing false teachings. God will judge that person, whoever he is, who has been confusing you.

Change is inevitable! Change is the evidence of life. Why not make it positive change. There are a few points I'd like to make regarding change:

1. Strengthen your focus. It's good to have options but sometimes, options are there to distract you. Don't focus on options if you know what God told you to do.
There are three P's to keep your focus:
Prayer – regular prayer is important for every believer.
Passion – make sure you're passionate about duty to the Lord
Power- you get power from the Holy Ghost

> **Acts 1:8 (NLT)** ⁸But you will receive power when the Holy Spirit comes upon you. And you will be my witnesses, telling people about me everywhere—in Jerusalem, throughout Judea, in Samaria, and to the ends of the earth."

2. Guard your spirit. The devil will send the same type of person that you are to distract you from your purpose. This why it's not good to be friends with someone with all the exact same dislikes. Your ability to grow is lessened.

Know methods and devices of enemy. The devil will trick you with glamorous schemes and clever people. Everything that looks like opportunity is not of God.

    3. There are three types of people Satan uses to distract you:

- One with insight – they can see your potential
- Person with influence – people who has gained your trust. Some of these people have influence but not integrity.
- People that use intimidation. You have to really watch out for these people. Unfortunately, some of us work for or have worked for people like this.

> **Isaiah 50:4 (NLT)** ⁴ The Sovereign LORD has given me his words of wisdom, so that I know how to comfort the weary. Morning by morning he wakens me and opens my understanding to his will.

We need to be willful and obedient children of the Lord. We should daily seek the Lords will for our lives. He is the one that gives us joy. Joy is an intense happiness not associated with circumstances.

You've all heard the expression about keeping up with the Jones' or running with the Jones. Don't run with Jones, run to Jesus! We need a rebirth in our own lives and Jesus will give us a fresh new start.

We should celebrate the Giver. Acknowledge in all you have and you will be blessed. If you need something, praise God even before you're blessed. Find the joy in your experiences.

A critical area needed in every Christian life is faith! Faith is the key to everything we do for it is faith that will keep us looking for and having hope in God's promises.

> **Hebrews 11:1 (NLT)** ¹Faith is the confidence that what we hope for will actually happen; it gives us assurance about things we cannot see.

> **Hebrews 11:6 (NLT)** ⁶And it is impossible to please God without faith. Anyone who wants to come to him must believe that God exists and that he rewards those who sincerely seek him.

Don't make every prayer be about materialistic things and don't make prayer always about you. Don't get me wrong, there is nothing wrong in having things. Just don't let obtaining things be the full focus of your prayers. God is not concerned with how much you have but how much of Him you have.

> **2 Corinthians 1:20-22 (NLT)** [20]For all of God's promises have been fulfilled in Christ with a resounding "Yes!" And through Christ, our "Amen" (which means "Yes") ascends to God for his glory. [21]It is God who enables us, along with you, to stand firm for Christ. He has commissioned us, [22]and he has identified us as his own by placing the Holy Spirit in our hearts as the first installment that guarantees everything he has promised us.

The devil will put your faith to test. Be prepared to face some challenges in your life. Throughout any test, stay in faith! If God told you something and you know it was God, God will not go against His word. I don't ever want to make a move unless the Lord says it's okay to do something. When God is ready to deliver you from your trials, you have to be ready! Have the wisdom to know that having faith in God is the only way to go. Without faith it's impossible to please God.

> **Romans 4:13 - 17 (NLT)** [13]Clearly, God's promise to give the whole earth to Abraham and his descendants was based not on his obedience to God's law, but on a right relationship with God that comes

by faith. ¹⁴If God's promise is only for those who obey the law, then faith is not necessary and the promise is pointless. ¹⁵For the law always brings punishment on those who try to obey it. (The only way to avoid breaking the law is to have no law to break!) ¹⁶So the promise is received by faith. It is given as a free gift. And we are all certain to receive it, whether or not we live according to the law of Moses, if we have faith like Abraham's. For Abraham is the father of all who believe. ¹⁷That is what the Scriptures mean when God told him, "I have made you the father of many nations." This happened because Abraham believed in the God who brings the dead back to life and who creates new things out of nothing.

With Godly Wisdom Comes Favor

God blesses his children with favor! The Bible said we have not because we ask not (James 4:2-3). Since some of us don't know the favor of God, we don't ask for much since we don't think we would ever get it. We focus too much on our meager means and don't realize that God is capable of doing anything for you that He pleases. Be careful of your motives for what you're asking God for and always give Him the glory.

> **Psalms 106:13-15 (NLT)** 13 Yet how quickly they forgot what he had done! They wouldn't wait for his counsel! 14 In the wilderness their desires ran wild, testing God's patience in that dry wasteland. 15 So he gave them what they asked for, but he sent a plague along with it.

If we follow the Lord, we will never lack. I've heard the expression, "Don't let your toys make too much noise". This means that you should not brag on your possessions or use them to make others look bad. Also, don't be flashy with your blessings. Remain humble and gracious to God no matter what. Remember, one who kneels to the Lord can stand up to anything!

Keep God's praise in your mouth! Pray to Him daily and often. Prayer and praise equals recovery. Prayer also brings about freedom.

P – Praise the Lord
R – Repent of your sins
A – Ask for yourself and others
Y – Yield yourself to God's will

There is another acronym called PUSH (Pray until something happens). This applies to everything you do in life.

> **Psalms 37:7 (NLT)** 7 Be still in the presence of the LORD, and wait patiently for him to act. Don't worry about evil people who prosper or fret about their wicked schemes.

Heb. 11:1 provides a great description of what faith is.

> **Hebrews 11:1 (NLT)** 1Faith is the confidence that what we hope for will actually happen; it gives us assurance about things we cannot see.

You must walk right in the light of the Lord, not just talk about it. Faith ignites favor. God has given us a foretaste of things getting ready to happen. You may not see it but God's fingerprint is all over your situation.

> **Romans 8:18 (NLT)** ¹⁸Yet what we suffer now is nothing compared to the glory he will reveal to us later.

With favor, you should forget about the disappointments of your past. Try to put it all behind you and look forward to a bright future in the Lord. God's favor will enable you to do things beyond how much money you have, influence you possess, and your physical ability.

> **Joshua 3:5 (NLT)** ⁵Then Joshua told the people, "Purify yourselves, for tomorrow the LORD will do great wonders among you."

Midnight begins a new night. You should get excited about tomorrow. You never know in advance what the favor of God will bring your way daily.

> **Romans 8:31 (NLT)** ³¹What shall we say about such wonderful things as these? If God is for us, who can ever be against us?

This does not mean that people won't come against you. What it means is that no one can successfully come against you when God is for you! Tomorrow says there is still hope. You must tell yourself, "I'm coming out of 'not enough'. What you've done in the past does not always help get you to the future – you have to change some things. Once you get a vision of where you want to be, you have to write down the vision!

The Beginning of Favor

One of favorite stories of God's favor is in Genesis 39:20 when Joseph was falsely thrown in prison.

> **Genesis 39:20 - 21 (NLT)** [20]So he took Joseph and threw him into the prison where the king's prisoners were held, and there he remained. [21]But the LORD was with Joseph in the prison and showed him his faithful love. And the LORD made Joseph a favorite with the prison warden.

This story illustrates how in the times of trouble, God is setting you up for a blessing! We never know what God is up to. In Joseph's case, God was setting Joseph up to be noticed by the right person. Joseph later gained more than he lost from his imprisonment. In your case, God will cause those that were previously against you to show you kindness and favor. You won't have to fight them for what you need.

> **Exodus 3:20 - 21 (NLT)** [20]So I will raise my hand and strike the Egyptians, performing all kinds of miracles among them. Then at last he will let you go. [21]And I will cause the Egyptians to look

> favorably on you. They will give you gifts when you go so you will not leave empty-handed.

God can show you favor directly and through people.

> **1 Samuel 2:26 (NLT)** ²⁶Meanwhile, the boy Samuel grew taller and grew in favor with the LORD and with the people.

1 Samuel 16:22 discussed how David had favor with the king. This is also a case of how your servitude can lead to leadership. The king later put David in a position of power.

> **1 Samuel 16:22 - 23 (NLT)** ²²Then Saul sent word to Jesse asking, "Please let David remain in my service, for I am very pleased with him." ²³And whenever the tormenting spirit from God troubled Saul, David would play the harp. Then Saul would feel better, and the tormenting spirit would go away.

Through the spirit of God, David helped Saul through his troubled moments. This is similar to how Esther gained favor from King Xerxes.

Empowered By Wisdom

> **Esther 5:2 - 3 (NLT)** ²When he saw Queen Esther standing there in the inner court, he welcomed her and held out the gold scepter to her. So Esther approached and touched the end of the scepter. ³Then the king asked her, "What do you want, Queen Esther? What is your request? I will give it to you, even if it is half the kingdom!"

Esther wasn't selfish. She used her favor with the king to help her people. Mordecai came to Esther for help when he found out about Haman's plot to kill the Jews.

> **Esther 5:8 (NLT)** ⁸If I have found favor with the king, and if it pleases the king to grant my request and do what I ask, please come with Haman tomorrow to the banquet I will prepare for you. Then I will explain what this is all about."

Haman saw Mordecai as a threat so he plotted to have King Xerxes kill Mordecai. Through Esther's help, Haman was exposed and was killed by the trap he set for Mordecai. God's favor will save you from the snares your enemies set for you. Psalms 30:5 shows His favor is life!

Empowered By Wisdom

> **Psalms 30:4-5 (NLT)** ⁴ Sing to the LORD, all you godly ones! Praise his holy name. ⁵ For his anger lasts only a moment, but his favor lasts a lifetime! Weeping may last through the night, but joy comes with the morning.

Let's face it, there are things in our lives that will hurt and cause us to cry. After all, we are human after all. The point of all this is not that we won't ever have to cry. The point is God will bless us out of our disappointments and one day, we will rejoice.

> **Proverbs 3:5-6 (NLT)** ⁵ Trust in the LORD with all your heart; do not depend on your own understanding. ⁶ Seek his will in all you do, and he will show you which path to take.

Regardless of your disappointments, keep your faith in God. You may be quite capable of handling many problems in life on your own. Efforts we take on our own are temporary and fleeting. God's work is positive and it's permanent! Don't take too much stock in your own understand of how things should work out.

> **Proverbs 3:7 (NLT)** ⁷ Don't be impressed with your own wisdom.

> Instead, fear the LORD and turn away from evil.

Always be willing to listen to what God is telling you. You gain much favor by abiding in God's will and seeking his ways.

> **Proverbs 8:34-35 (NLT)** ³⁴ Joyful are those who listen to me, watching for me daily at my gates, waiting for me outside my home! ³⁵ For whoever finds me finds life and receives favor from the LORD.

Be wise enough to know you have to treat all of God's creation with respect. Stop thinking you're so much better than everyone else and remain humble with your blessings. Don't rejoice in another person's demise and never be a part of a plan to mistreat another person, whether alone or with someone else.

> **Proverbs 12:2 (NLT)** ² The LORD approves of those who are good, but he condemns those who plan wickedness.

Take heed to the advice of those who are older than you and those who have more experience than you, regardless of their age. However, beware that God can speak to you through younger people, those less experienced than you, and other unlikely people.

> **Proverbs 13:13-14 (NLT)** [13] People who despise advice are asking for trouble; those who respect a command will succeed. [14] The instruction of the wise is like a life-giving fountain; those who accept it avoid the snares of death.

No matter where you are in life or what you're doing, always seek wise counsel. Beware of whom you seek counsel though for the devil is out to trap you with important looking or people who sound like they have a lot of knowledge. Watch with whom you keep counsel with. Watch what you say to others and what you say about other people. I told my son to beware of sweet looking women with bitter souls. I told him that as a father, there were a lot of things I can do for him; however, through prayer he will have to find the right wife on his own.

> **Proverbs 18:20-22 (NLT)** [20] Wise words satisfy like a good meal; the right words bring satisfaction. [21] The tongue can bring death or life; those who love to talk will reap the consequences. [22] The man who finds a wife finds a treasure, and he receives favor from the LORD.

Some people like to lie to get what they want. Don't ever compromise your reputation by lying to get the things you want. Wouldn't it be a sad day when you get that big thing you wanted or the promotion you thought you deserved and then not have anyone to share it with or someone to sincerely congratulate you for your success?

> **Proverbs 22:1 (NLT)** ¹ Choose a good reputation over great riches; being held in high esteem is better than silver or gold.

Sometimes stepping out on faith after God tells you to do something can be a scary thing. We have to deny fear and do what God tells us. Even if the results don't end up being what you wanted or the action you took wasn't successful, God could be testing you to see if you will act when he tells you to do something else in the future. There is not always an instant reward when we do what God tells us to do. Even Mary was afraid at first.

> **Luke 1:30 (NLT)** ³⁰"Don't be afraid, Mary," the angel told her, "for you have found favor with God!

No matter what level you are in life, never think that you possess all the wisdom you'll ever need. Even Jesus had to grow in wisdom.

Empowered By Wisdom

> **Luke 2:52 (NLT)** ⁵²Jesus grew in wisdom and in stature and in favor with God and all the people.

Continue to seek more wisdom as you live your life. You can never have too much wisdom. Give God the glory for all good things in your life. You should even praise Him when times are bad for it's the bad things that make you grow in faith.

> **Acts 2:47 (NLT)** ⁴⁷all the while praising God and enjoying the goodwill of all the people. And each day the Lord added to their fellowship those who were being saved.

Sometimes you will question your own faith. Don't worry we all are human and will sometimes question God concerning things in our lives we don't understand. Stand strong in the Lord and He will continue to bless you.

> **Joshua 1:9 (NLT)** ⁹This is my command—be strong and courageous! Do not be afraid or discouraged. For the LORD your God is with you wherever you go."

Don't listen to those that don't believe in God or weak Christians who don't have a personal relationship with God and says God don't talk to us. God speaks to us in different ways. Many ways you can hear God's voice speaking to you and at other times it's just a solid feeling you're on the right track on things you're doing or are about to do. Keeping in tune with God's Will makes you stronger and helps you disregard negative messages from others and take heed to reassurances from God.

> **Psalms 1:1-3 (NLT)** ¹ Oh, the joys of those who do not follow the advice of the wicked, or stand around with sinners, or join in with mockers. ² But they delight in the law of the LORD, meditating on it day and night. ³ They are like trees planted along the riverbank, bearing fruit each season. Their leaves never wither, and they prosper in all they do.

Empowered By Wisdom

Devine Favor

I believe that all favor is from God. We discussed what I call the beginning of favor. That is simply God working things for you without much fuss. The next level of favor is what I call Devine favor. This sort of favor happens when things are somewhat against you but God turns it all around. Receive not what the world is saying but what God is saying. God will protect you from the things that happen to you.

> **Psalms 5:11-12 (NLT)** [11] But let all who take refuge in you rejoice; let them sing joyful praises forever. Spread your protection over them, that all who love your name may be filled with joy. [12] For you bless the godly, O LORD; you surround them with your shield of love.

I've said on many occasions that being a Christian does not mean you won't face problems. Sometimes you will fail at some things or situations. You may fail many times but I encourage you to be strong and keep turning to the Lord.

> **Proverbs 24:16-17 (NLT)** [16] The godly may trip seven times, but they will get up again. But one disaster is enough to overthrow the wicked. [17] Don't rejoice

when your enemies fall; don't be happy when they stumble.

When you get in line with God's will, your failing days are over, get ready to succeed! God will bless you in ways unimaginable. Being blessed means being empowered and becoming prosperous. Read God's word and try to be righteous. God blesses the righteous. One problem with being righteous is that the Bible says all people are sinners.

> **Romans 3:10 (NLT)** 10As the Scriptures say, "No one is righteous — not even one.

We all have come short of doing everything God wants us to do. Don't despair, God forgives us of our sins and wants us to turn to him.

> **Romans 3:23-24 (NLT)** 23For everyone has sinned; we all fall short of God's glorious standard. 24Yet God, with undeserved kindness, declares that we are righteous. He did this through Christ Jesus when he freed us from the penalty for our sins.

I have known throughout my life that there are some good people out there. Unfortunately, being good is not the only thing that will get you into heaven. You have to come to know and acknowledge God. There are some out there who think they will go to heaven simply due to all the nice deeds they've done. Sometimes these deeds have ulterior or wrong motives. Don't count on your good deeds to get you to heaven. You need salvation!

> **Romans 4:2-3 (NLT)** 2If his good deeds had made him acceptable to God, he would have had something to boast about. But that was not God's way. 3For the Scriptures tell us, "Abraham believed God, and God counted him as righteous because of his faith."

I have learned along my life's path that as Christians we are the seed of Abraham. Abraham was a faithful man and God blessed him and his family immensely. Since we are Abraham's heir, you should live a blessed life. Seek the righteousness of God and you too can have the blessings of Abraham.

> **Romans 4:23 - 24 (NLT)** 23And when God counted him as righteous, it wasn't just for Abraham's benefit. It was recorded 24for our benefit, too, assuring us that God will also count us as

righteous if we believe in him, the one who raised Jesus our Lord from the dead.

It was Abraham's faith that made him so blessed! You must have just as much faith to receive God's promises. Faith is one of the biggest demands God placed on us. You must faith in Him and Him only. God sometimes works through people to bless you. When a person helps you there is nothing wrong with thanking them. You should also thank God for placing that person in your path to bless you. Seek God's guidance in all you do.

> **Hebrews 11:6 (NLT)** 6And it is impossible to please God without faith. Anyone who wants to come to him must believe that God exists and that he rewards those who sincerely seek him.

Christ came to earth to let people know that there is only one true God. Although he never committed a sin, Christ was persecuted and later crucified for our sin. Believe in Christ and you will be saved from you sin, no matter what it is.

> **2 Corinthians 5:21 (NLT)** 21For God made Christ, who never sinned, to be the

> offering for our sin, so that we could be
> made right with God through Christ.

When you gain the faith I have been talking about, God will give you favor in your daily life. If you didn't know, favor is a friendly or kind regard. Favor causes 'unfair' treatment to flow. This unfair treatment is positive in nature. It's a good thing and nothing negative.

In order to keep favor in your life you may need to change the people in your environment. There are three kinds of people you need in your life:

1) Those that add to your life. These could be friends, coworkers, neighbors or your spouse.

2) Those that protect your life. These cold be the same group of people but with more special attention to your benefits.

3) Those that correct you. These must be people you can trust. You can't take advice or instruction from just anyone. Ask God about these people so you can know who you can listen to.

Supernatural Favor

Supernatural favor is super abundance that comes from a supernatural source. These are the kinds of miraculous things that people can't always explain. This is also the kind of favor that shelters you from your bad habits that are hard to break! Like me, you should say Lord, I need your supernatural favor! Each year you should start the year with more than you ever had. That would include faith and joy. One day of favor can do more for you than a lifetime of work. – Mike Murdoch

> **Psalms 5:12 (NLT)** [12] For you bless the godly, O LORD; you surround them with your shield of love.

As a Christian you must have faith and endurance. Trials will come your way and you must not lose your faith in God and his ability to help you in all situations. James 1:2 says we should count it all joy the things we have to go through.

> **James 1:2 (NLT)** [2] Dear brothers and sisters, when troubles come your way, consider it an opportunity for great joy.

The faithful will enjoy favor as they go through trials and tribulations. You should say to yourself, "Favor, it's on me and it's not my fault". Psalms 90:17 talks about the favor of God.

> **Psalms 90:17 (NLT)** 17 And may the Lord our God show us his approval and make our efforts successful. Yes, make our efforts successful!

When he have to fight battles, Ephesians 6:10, 11 says we have to put on the full armor of God.

> **Ephesians 6:10 - 11 (NLT)** 10A final word: Be strong in the Lord and in his mighty power. 11Put on all of God's armor so that you will be able to stand firm against all strategies of the devil.

Weak relationships with God produces a weak shield. We have to strengthen our relationships with God in order to access all the favor available. Favor is not an accident. We have to work to get this unmerited favor. Even though some of us may work hard for the favor of God, we still can't do enough to deserve it. God's favor gives us power.

> **2 Chronicles 1:1 (NLT)** ¹Solomon son of David took firm control of his kingdom, for the LORD his God was with him and made him very powerful.

We Christians are human, but we don't wage physical war as other humans do. 2 Corinthians 10:5 discusses Spiritual weapons.

> **2 Corinthians 10:4-5 (NLT)** ⁴ We use God's mighty weapons, not worldly weapons, to knock down the strongholds of human reasoning and to destroy false arguments. ⁵ We destroy every proud obstacle that keeps people from knowing God. We capture their rebellious thoughts and teach them to obey Christ.

There are tools we can use to tap into God's goodness. One of the tools is fasting. Fasting is a tool where God can do something extraordinary. Remember, the battle is the Lord's. We have to rely on Him to fight our battles.

When we are looking for God to deliver us, praise God before the manifestation of your blessing. Praise God and His Glory will be revealed. We must continue to worship Him regardless of your situation. Worship leads to victory. Praise will catapult you into a glorified promise.

Through family or church members' families I have heard how God had supernaturally delivered people from cancer. Some with treatment and many without doctors' intervention. Even the doctors treating these people were amazed how God completely eliminated cancer from these people's bodies.

We need to look to God for all our needs!

> **1 Chronicles 29:11-14 (NLT)** [11] Yours, O LORD, is the greatness, the power, the glory, the victory, and the majesty. Everything in the heavens and on earth is yours, O LORD, and this is your kingdom. We adore you as the one who is over all things. [12] Wealth and honor come from you alone, for you rule over everything. Power and might are in your hand, and at your discretion people are made great and given strength. [13] "O our God, we thank you and praise your glorious name! [14] But who am I, and who are my people, that we could give anything to you? Everything we have has come from you, and we give you only what you first gave us!

Sometimes we will wonder if God is paying attention to our needs. When we pray, we should know God hears us. Some of the things we seek are not for us and that's why they don't happen. God always have something better in mind. Unfortunately for us, God's timing is not our timing. Philippians 4:6 tells us to not be anxious for anything.

> **Philippians 4:6 (NLT)** 6Don't worry about anything; instead, pray about everything. Tell God what you need, and thank him for all he has done.

I highly recommend you to stop worrying, God is in control! God has meaning to everything you're going through.

> *Amos 3:6 (NLT) 6 When the ram's horn blows a warning, shouldn't the people be alarmed? Does disaster come to a city unless the LORD has planned it?*

I have learned at one point in life to not worry about anything, and pray about everything. You should give God thanks in advance.

> **Romans 8:26 (NLT)** 26And the Holy Spirit helps us in our weakness. For example, we don't know what God wants us to pray for. But the Holy Spirit prays for us with groanings that cannot be expressed in words.

I have learned that God will make all things work together for the good. Romans 8:28 discusses how all things work for the better.

> **Romans 8:28 (NLT)** ²⁸And we know that God causes everything to work together for the good of those who love God and are called according to his purpose for them.

One of the reasons we worry is that we can only see our current situation that's before us. We can see our "now", but God can see our future. There's a story in the Bible where God knew the people's future but they could only see their current situation. God gave the Israelites the command to leave Sinai and they wondered why.

> **Deuteronomy 1:5 - 8 (NLT)** ⁵ While the Israelites were in the land of Moab east of the Jordan River, Moses carefully explained the LORD's instructions as follows. ⁶ "When we were at Mount Sinai, the LORD our God said to us, 'You have stayed at this mountain long enough. ⁷ It is time to break camp and move on. Go to the hill country of the Amorites and to all the neighboring regions—the Jordan Valley, the hill

> country, the western foothills, the Negev, and the coastal plain. Go to the land of the Canaanites and to Lebanon, and all the way to the great Euphrates River. ⁸ Look, I am giving all this land to you! Go in and occupy it, for it is the land the LORD swore to give to your ancestors Abraham, Isaac, and Jacob, and to all their descendants.'"

God is taking us to the next level. I have witnessed how God will take us out of our comfort zone. Believe me when I say there is a blessing waiting for you! The Bible teaches us to trust the Lord.

> **Proverbs 3:1-2 (NLT)** ¹ My child, never forget the things I have taught you. Store my commands in your heart. ² If you do this, you will live many years, and your life will be satisfying.

I encourage each of you to be a part of a church that will help you grow spiritually. The church helps us make Godly decisions and find solutions to life situations. You must pray for the church and your pastor.

I strongly encourage you to get rid of accepting failure. Failure in life's situations happen but it does not mean you are a failure. You should increase your spiritual walk along with your physical walk. If you want to be successful, change your thinking. This is why wisdom is so important.

> **Proverbs 4:7 (NLT)** ⁷ Getting wisdom is the wisest thing you can do! And whatever else you do, develop good judgment.

Use Wisdom to See Yourself in God's Eyes

Christ came to earth to save us from ourselves. You must believe He bled and died for us. The truth about the blood is that it has everlasting power! I encourage you to get as much wisdom and knowledge that you can get. This could come from education, experience, prayer, and regularly reading the Bible. You can't expect all knowledge to come from just one source, unless your source is God-inspired.

> **Ephesians 1:16-20 (NLT)** [16] I have not stopped thanking God for you. I pray for you constantly, [17] asking God, the glorious Father of our Lord Jesus Christ, to give you spiritual wisdom and insight so that you might grow in your knowledge of God. [18] I pray that your hearts will be flooded with light so that you can understand the confident hope he has given to those he called—his holy people who are his rich and glorious inheritance. [19] I also pray that you will understand the incredible greatness of God's power for us who believe him. This is the same mighty power [20] that raised Christ from the dead and seated him in the place of honor at God's right hand in the heavenly realms.

Empowered By Wisdom

The Bible said Jehoshaphat stood before the community of Judah and Jerusalem at the Temple of the LORD and told the people to have faith in God.

> **2 Chronicles 20:6 (NLT)** ⁶He prayed, "O LORD, God of our ancestors, you alone are the God who is in heaven. You are ruler of all the kingdoms of the earth. You are powerful and mighty; no one can stand against you!

The Spirit of the LORD came upon Jahaziel, son of Zechariah, and he told the people God didn't want them to be afraid.

> **2 Chronicles 20:15 (NLT)** ¹⁵He said, "Listen, all you people of Judah and Jerusalem! Listen, King Jehoshaphat! This is what the LORD says: Do not be afraid! Don't be discouraged by this mighty army, for the battle is not yours, but God's.

In today's society you have information and news coming to you from many sources. Other than human contact you also have 24-hour news channels, social networking, cellular phones, portable tablets, and text messages. You have to watch out for the news being brought to you. You really must check out the messenger! Some of the people giving you information are either ignorant of the harm from the information or are operating with wrong motives. You have to say enough is enough!

> **Proverbs 17:16-24 (NLT)** 16 It is senseless to pay tuition to educate a fool, since he has no heart for learning. 17 A friend is always loyal, and a brother is born to help in time of need. 18 It's poor judgment to guarantee another person's debt or put up security for a friend. 19 Anyone who loves to quarrel loves sin; anyone who trusts in high walls invites disaster. 20 The crooked heart will not prosper; the lying tongue tumbles into trouble. 21 It is painful to be the parent of a fool; there is no joy for the father of a rebel. 22 A cheerful heart is good medicine, but a broken spirit saps a person's strength. 23 The wicked take secret bribes to pervert the course of justice. 24 Sensible people keep their eyes glued on wisdom, but a fool's eyes wander to the ends of the earth.

Keep yourself in daily prayer! While you're praying for things or situations, you choose also have a prayer of praise! You should thank God for the things you do have and ask that He bless you to be able to take care of them.

Empowered By Wisdom

Give all the glory to God.

> **Jude 1:24-25 (NLT)** 24Now all glory to God, who is able to keep you from falling away and will bring you with great joy into his glorious presence without a single fault. 25All glory to him who alone is God, our Savior through Jesus Christ our Lord. All glory, majesty, power, and authority are his before all time, and in the present, and beyond all time! Amen.

You give what the Bible calls the Benediction Blessing. Keep in mind that God is good and His Word is effective! You may be concerned about how other people receive you when you talk about how good God has been to you. Be aware that Jesus was rejected at Nazareth. Matthew 13:54, said the people asked "Where does he get this wisdom and the power to do miracles?" Since they didn't have an answer they assumed the worse and did not believe in him.

> **Mark 6:3 (NLT)** 3Then they scoffed, "He's just a carpenter, the son of Mary and the brother of James, Joseph, Judas, and Simon. And his sisters live right here among us." They were deeply offended and refused to believe in him.

Empowered By Wisdom

John 7:5 said, "For even his brothers didn't believe in him." Jude did not initially believe in his brother, Jesus. In your world, genuine encounters with Jesus gives new evangelism in you. One of the great blessing in life is to know which battles are worth fighting. Benediction of blessings has already been pronounced on your life. God is able! God is able to present you faultless.

Colossians discusses knowledge:

> **Colossians 2:1-4 (NLT)** ¹I want you to know how much I have agonized for you and for the church at Laodicea, and for many other believers who have never met me personally. ²I want them to be encouraged and knit together by strong ties of love. I want them to have complete confidence that they understand God's mysterious plan, which is Christ himself. ³In him lie hidden all the treasures of wisdom and knowledge. ⁴I am telling you this so no one will deceive you with well-crafted arguments.

Proverbs 8 said that wisdom calls for a hearing:

> **Proverbs 8:1-5 (NLT)** ¹ Listen as Wisdom calls out! Hear as understanding raises her voice! ² On the hilltop along

> the road, she takes her stand at the crossroads. ³ By the gates at the entrance to the town, on the road leading in, she cries aloud, ⁴ "I call to you, to all of you! I raise my voice to all people. ⁵ You simple people, use good judgment. You foolish people, show some understanding.

I encourage you to not turn your ear to instruction.

> **Proverbs 9:8-10 (NLT)** ⁸ So don't bother correcting mockers; they will only hate you. But correct the wise, and they will love you. ⁹ Instruct the wise, and they will be even wiser. Teach the righteous, and they will learn even more. ¹⁰ Fear of the LORD is the foundation of wisdom. Knowledge of the Holy One results in good judgment.

The Bible also says that folly calls for a hearing:

> **Proverbs 9:13-17 (NLT)** ¹³ The woman named Folly is brash. She is ignorant and doesn't know it. ¹⁴ She sits in her doorway on the heights overlooking the city. ¹⁵ She calls out to men going by who

> are minding their own business. ¹⁶ "Come in with me," she urges the simple. To those who lack good judgment, she says, ¹⁷ "Stolen water is refreshing; food eaten in secret tastes the best!"

Wisdom is something you should always seek. Jesus tried to tell us to have the wisdom to know that all things that happen to or with you is not always about you. Some things happen so God can show you how He works.

> **John 9:1 - 5 (NLT)** ¹As Jesus was walking along, he saw a man who had been blind from birth. ²"Rabbi," his disciples asked him, "why was this man born blind? Was it because of his own sins or his parents' sins?" ³"It was not because of his sins or his parents' sins," Jesus answered. "This happened so the power of God could be seen in him. ⁴We must quickly carry out the tasks assigned us by the one who sent us. The night is coming, and then no one can work. ⁵But while I am here in the world, I am the light of the world."

There is always a blessing in following instruction. People think obedience is belittling, not so! Deut. 28:1-8 tells us to do what the Lord says, and we will be blessed.

> **Deuteronomy 28:1-8 (NLT)** ¹"If you fully obey the LORD your God and carefully keep all his commands that I am giving you today, the LORD your God will set you high above all the nations of the world. ²You will experience all these blessings if you obey the LORD your God: ³ Your towns and your fields will be blessed. ⁴ Your children and your crops will be blessed. The offspring of your herds and flocks will be blessed. ⁵ Your fruit baskets and breadboards will be blessed. ⁶ Wherever you go and whatever you do, you will be blessed. ⁷ "The LORD will conquer your enemies when they attack you. They will attack you from one direction, but they will scatter from you in seven! ⁸ "The LORD will guarantee a blessing on everything you do and will fill your storehouses with grain. The LORD your God will bless you in the land he is giving you.

Many of us who have enjoyed success in anything we've done in the past have a tendency to think we only have to listen to our own voices and our own intentions. If you didn't know it already, no matter how close your relationship with God, He has placed persons in positions in good churches and we need to listen to what they have to say. God provides us messages from teachers and preachers in Bible-based churches where their heart is truly to seek God's will. Don't turn your ear to guidance and instructions.

> **Hebrews 13:17 (NLT)** ¹⁷Obey your spiritual leaders, and do what they say. Their work is to watch over your souls, and they are accountable to God. Give them reason to do this with joy and not with sorrow. That would certainly not be for your benefit.

If you are a part of a good church or should you later find one, rest assure the devil will try to attack you and have you thinking you should not be there. Use the things you learn in church to go out and live the life God wants you to lead. Don't get me wrong, it won't always be easy. You will sometimes find people will attack you just because who you're representing (Christ). God will provide you the wisdom to deal with these people and situations.

> **Luke 21:12-15 (NLT)** ¹²"But before all this occurs, there will be a time of great persecution. You will be dragged into synagogues and prisons, and you will stand trial before kings and governors because you are my followers. ¹³But this will be your opportunity to tell them about me. ¹⁴So don't worry in advance

about how to answer the charges against you, ¹⁵for I will give you the right words and such wisdom that none of your opponents will be able to reply or refute you!

It's sad for me to tell you that as a believer, there are folks out there planning your demise. You will ask yourself why people are attacking you when you've done nothing to attack them. They will taunt you just because of who you are (a Christian). Even if you don't preach or judge them, some of them won't like your disposition because you're being nice or act differently makes them jealous and they will not want to like you. Don't worry about this for in the Bible days, King Herod planned an attack on Jesus. Just like some people in your life, King Herod pretended to look for Jesus to honor him.

Matthew 2:1-9 (NLT) ¹ Jesus was born in Bethlehem in Judea, during the reign of King Herod. About that time some wise men from eastern lands arrived in Jerusalem, asking, ² "Where is the newborn king of the Jews? We saw his star as it rose, and we have come to worship him." ³ King Herod was deeply disturbed when he heard this, as was everyone in Jerusalem. ⁴ He called a meeting of the leading priests and teachers of religious law and asked, "Where is the Messiah supposed to be

> born?" ⁵ "In Bethlehem in Judea," they said, "for this is what the prophet wrote: ⁶ 'And you, O Bethlehem in the land of Judah, are not least among the ruling cities of Judah, for a ruler will come from you who will be the shepherd for my people Israel.'" ⁷ Then Herod called for a private meeting with the wise men, and he learned from them the time when the star first appeared. ⁸ Then he told them, "Go to Bethlehem and search carefully for the child. And when you find him, come back and tell me so that I can go and worship him, too!" ⁹ After this interview the wise men went their way. And the star they had seen in the east guided them to Bethlehem. It went ahead of them and stopped over the place where the child was.

King Herod had an ulterior motive to locate Jesus. He wanted to kill Jesus! If you have a personal relationship with God, He will speak to you in different ways. One way is that God will warn you in a dream, just as he did with Joseph.

> **Matthew 2:13 - 15 (NLT)** ¹³ After the wise men were gone, an angel of the Lord appeared to Joseph in a dream. "Get up! Flee to Egypt with the child and his mother," the angel said. "Stay there until

> I tell you to return, because Herod is going to search for the child to kill him." 14 That night Joseph left for Egypt with the child and Mary, his mother, 15 and they stayed there until Herod's death. This fulfilled what the Lord had spoken through the prophet: "I called my Son out of Egypt."

God will guide you in your daily walk. Most of you remember the story of Jesus' birth and how the wise men followed a star to his location. Are you aware it was the glory of Jesus that shined the star, and it was not the other way around? That's a good thing. God's word gives us courage and not dismay. There's nothing sad about God's Word. When God is for you, your nights will become days. Rachel was an example in the Bible of how God can turn sadness to joy.

> **Jeremiah 31:15-18 (NLT)** 15 This is what the LORD says: "A cry is heard in Ramah — deep anguish and bitter weeping. Rachel weeps for her children, refusing to be comforted — for her children are gone." 16 But now this is what the LORD says: "Do not weep any longer, for I will reward you," says the LORD. "Your children will come back to you from the distant land of the enemy. 17 There is hope for your future," says the LORD. "Your children will

> come again to their own land. ⁱ⁸ I have heard Israel saying, 'You disciplined me severely, like a calf that needs training for the yoke. Turn me again to you and restore me, for you alone are the LORD my God.

All too often, people want to label you a statistic based on your circumstances. Don't focus on your circumstances or being labeled. When folks want to label you as a statistic, God will show you're a miracle! If you look over your life you should realize how God has blessed you to be where you are, even if you're not yet where you want to be. Just tell God, "Lord, Do It Again!" If you pay attention and take head to what God tells you, God will bless you and make your paths clear!

> **Mark 8:25 (NLT)** ²⁵Then Jesus placed his hands on the man's eyes again, and his eyes were opened. His sight was completely restored, and he could see everything clearly.

You should continually seek God's will and His Word. People are looking for miracles but not the Word. You should read God's Word regularly. Every now and then, we all need a second touch. You should need God every day. God is Jehovah Jireh, He will provide.

Empowered By Wisdom

When God provides for you, you won't be turning heads, but breaking necks! People who know you will wonder how you were able to do the things you've done or get a certain thing (money, houses, cars) when they knew you had no money or had bad credit.

When God gets you straight you should understand that God has broken something inside you in order for you to get right. You need to consecrate yourself. Do listen to what God tells you. Don't be stubborn by not doing what the Lord tells you to do. We have to break the spirit off some things in our lives and homes. The first neck to break in church is false identity. Don't pretend to be something you're not and stop putting on false faces.

You will have to breach the neck of poverty. God don't want us to be poor but if you are, thank God for what you have, take care of it, and He will provide more when He knows you can handle it. While I'm on this, we need to break the spirit of irresponsibility. How can you expect God to bless you with money or things when you don't appreciate nor take care of the things and people that are currently in your life?

Regardless of the pushback you get from talking about your love for Christ, never be ashamed of who you are or whose you are. When it comes to your faith and belief, are you in the closet? Don't be. This does not mean you have to make all your praise and worship public. You don't have to put on a show to demonstrate your Christianity.

> **Matthew 6:5-6 (NLT)** ⁵ "When you pray, don't be like the hypocrites who love to pray publicly on street corners and in the synagogues where everyone can see them. I tell you the truth, that is all the reward they will ever get. ⁶ But when you pray, go away by yourself, shut the door behind you, and pray to your Father in private. Then your Father, who sees everything, will reward you.

I hope you know God sees everything you do. You can fool people about who you are and what you do in private, but God is never fooled. Stop living a life that is not unto the Lord. You should come out of your worldly closet and into God's closet. There are good things about God's secret closet. Again, that means you have to read God's words often. You also have to shut some things out of your life. You'll find that God's love is unfailing and he will protect you.

> **Psalms 17:7-9 (NLT)** ⁷ Show me your unfailing love in wonderful ways. By your mighty power you rescue those who seek refuge from their enemies. ⁸ Guard me as you would guard your own eyes. Hide me in the shadow of your wings. ⁹ Protect me from wicked people who attack me, from murderous enemies who surround me.

When trouble comes you should ask the Lord to hide you in his shadows. Some of us are crying out to the wrong people! There's nothing wrong with talking to a trusted friend about your problems or what you're going through; however, you should look to the Lord to carry you through your problems. Again I say you must never doubt that God can bring you through your problems, regardless of how hopeless your situation may seem. Your faith will be tried many times in life but never give up!

Our faithfulness is one of the most important things we need in our relationship with God. God only asked Adam and Eve to be faithful. God will faithfully fulfill any promise He's made to you. The way you respond to your problem will determine how you come out of your problem.

The parable of the lost son is yet one example of how if you come to God, He will deliver you. God knows you may lose your way in life. What matters is not how to you got to where you are, what matters is how you respond to the problem and to whom you run.

> **Luke 15:17 (NLT)** 17"When he finally came to his senses, he said to himself, 'At home even the hired servants have food enough to spare, and here I am dying of hunger!

Empowered By Wisdom

God blessed the lost son because he realized he made a mistake and he should go back to his father; not only his biological father but also his heavenly father. It's not what you're going through, but what you're going to that should motivate you. God has a glorious destination for you if you follow His lead! This will include members of your family. You should continue to show your family your faith in God and hopefully they will have faith as well.

> **Acts 16:31 (NLT)** 31They replied, "Believe in the Lord Jesus and you will be saved, along with everyone in your household."

Jesus suffered so you won't have to. Don't let his suffering in vain. He didn't die so you can be defeated by your enemies! Jesus knew what his fate would be even though he didn't understand why he was persecuted. Jesus looked to his father for answers just as we should look to Him.

> **Isaiah 53:5 (NLT)** 5 But he was pierced for our rebellion, crushed for our sins. He was beaten so we could be whole. He was whipped so we could be healed.

The same God that takes care of me is the same God that will take care of you. God shows his mercy to even those that don't believe in him. I think He does so in order that those persons that don't believe will one day realize it was God that made a way for them.

> **Philippians 4:19 (NLT)** ¹⁹And this same God who takes care of me will supply all your needs from his glorious riches, which have been given to us in Christ Jesus.

God wants to take each of us to special places in our lives. This place and direction of travel will be different for each of us. No two people's journey will be the same. I think that our choices we make and especially counting on God will determine when, how, and if we get to our destination. God has plans for us that we cannot even imagine.

> **Deuteronomy 6:10 (NLT)** ¹⁰"The LORD your God will soon bring you into the land he swore to give you when he made a vow to your ancestors Abraham, Isaac, and Jacob. It is a land with large, prosperous cities that you did not build.

We need to read "the good book" (Bible) often and allow God to show us passages that apply to us and our situations. Don't stop there; meditate on God's Word and ask Him how he wants you to use the knowledge and wisdom you gain in your reading.

> **Joshua 1:8 (NLT)** ⁸Study this Book of Instruction continually. Meditate on it day and night so you will be sure to obey everything written in it. Only then will you prosper and succeed in all you do.

Those that take heed to God's Word and His instructions will be blessed! You may have to take a detour occasionally but if you stay on the right track, you will eventually see what God was doing for you. There have been many times in my life where I wondered why God took me to the places and the situations I found myself in. Some of the purposes I may never know but I realized some of the reasons for my experiences later after God brought me out. All of your experiences don't have to be negative. God will bless us to be in the most wonderful places and we wonder how we got there.

> **Psalms 1:3 (NLT)** ³ They are like trees planted along the riverbank, bearing fruit each season. Their leaves never wither, and they prosper in all they do.

Not only do we need to connect with God spiritually, we need to also connect with him physically. We can do that by taking care of your bodily temple and representing Him in your daily walk. You don't have to wear the latest in fashion or be a part of newest trend to be noticed! When you're walking in the light of God, people are going to notice you. You should show your most radiant smile when you greet people. Some of them will wonder why you're smiling when they know you have personal problems you're dealing with.

> **3 John 1:2 (NLT)** ²Dear friend, I hope all is well with you and that you are as healthy in body as you are strong in spirit.

Too many of us have run from what God wanted us to do. Some of us may have finally sought His will but many are still running. If God is calling you to ministry, don't run from it. If God is calling for you to connect with a local church and be a part of a good ministry, listen to him. If God is telling you to move away from a certain group of people that are holding you back, don't be afraid to let them go. God will sometimes set conditions on you. You have to meet the conditions before you can receive the promise.

> **John 10:10 (NLT)** ¹⁰The thief's purpose is to steal and kill and destroy. My purpose is to give them a rich and satisfying life.

Some of the people you are trying to be like or that you idolize are not necessarily the ones to whom you should be looking. Some of these people are a bad influence on you or they won't be who you thought they were when you've gotten a little too close to them. Find the right people to associate yourself.

> **Proverbs 23:6-7 (NLT)** 6 Don't eat with people who are stingy; don't desire their delicacies. 7 They are always thinking about how much it costs. "Eat and drink," they say, but they don't mean it.

To have proper wisdom you have to have faith. Faith will take you beyond your means of doing things in your life. Just because you have a lot of money doesn't mean you can do all that you want. You, too, must turn to God for guidance.

> **Mark 11:24 (NLT)** 24 I tell you, you can pray for anything, and if you believe that you've received it, it will be yours.

God is good no matter what you're going through. Sometimes God will have you do things that don't turn out the way you thought they would. It's not always for us to understand why God will have us do a certain thing or talk to a certain person. You have to have blind faith in God and in no one else, even if you don't understand what's going on.

> **Hebrews 11:8 (NLT)** ⁸It was by faith that Abraham obeyed when God called him to leave home and go to another land that God would give him as his inheritance. He went without knowing where he was going.

Never question God's Word or His instructions. However, as I've mentioned before, you'd better know if it's God that's talking to you. God will never lead you to do evil things (such as killing someone without it being self-defense) or wrong things (such as sexual immorality).

> **2 Corinthians 1:19-20 (NLT)** ¹⁹ For Jesus Christ, the Son of God, does not waver between "Yes" and "No." He is the one whom Silas, Timothy, and I preached to you, and as God's ultimate "Yes," he always does what he says. ²⁰ For all of God's promises have been fulfilled in Christ with a resounding "Yes!" And through Christ, our "Amen" (which means "Yes") ascends to God for his glory.

Empowered By Wisdom

Sometimes you have to give up things of the past. This could include some family traditions that are wrong, bad habits, and long histories of family abuse. You have to be spiritually mature in your relationship with God and He will supply all your needs.

> **Psalms 37:25 (NLT)** 25 Once I was young, and now I am old. Yet I have never seen the godly abandoned or their children begging for bread.

Get closer to God and ask Him what His will is for your life. Discover the inner beauty and hidden talents that God has placed inside you. Once you get on the right road God wanted you to be on, don't look back to your past! Luke 9:62 tells us to not look back.

> **Luke 9:62 (NLT)** 62But Jesus told him, "Anyone who puts a hand to the plow and then looks back is not fit for the Kingdom of God."

You need to thank God for your victories even before they occur! This a sign of spiritual maturity and faith. Praise God for what He has done for you and for the things He will do. Don't stop the praise from victory to victory.

> **Psalms 100:2-3 (NLT)** ² Worship the LORD with gladness. Come before him, singing with joy. ³ Acknowledge that the LORD is God! He made us, and we are his. We are his people, the sheep of his pasture.

Your relationship with God should be beyond the material things you need and want. You should communicate with Him daily. God wants us to praise him for who He is and not for what we want. You will have regular communication with God and not just call on Him when you need something.

> **Luke 6:46-47 (NLT)** ⁴⁶ "So why do you keep calling me 'Lord, Lord!' when you don't do what I say? ⁴⁷ I will show you what it's like when someone comes to me, listens to my teaching, and then follows it.

Get ready for God to make you an example of a person living your life for the Lord. Be a willing, living sacrifice. Wake up each morning and thank God for seeing another day! Do your job as if it was unto the Lord!

> **Matthew 5:14-16 (NLT)** ¹⁴ "You are the light of the world—like a city on a hilltop

> that cannot be hidden. ¹⁵ No one lights a lamp and then puts it under a basket. Instead, a lamp is placed on a stand, where it gives light to everyone in the house. ¹⁶ In the same way, let your good deeds shine out for all to see, so that everyone will praise your heavenly Father.

You should be willing to shine the light that's within you as Jesus did as he walked along the earth. When Jesus healed a man born blind his disciples asked him questions about why he did what he did. John 9:5 tells us that Jesus told his disciples he was the light of the world.

> **John 9:5 (NLT)** ⁵ But while I am here in the world, I am the light of the world."

What most of this boils down to is that Jesus is the son of God and we must see him as our Lord and savior. God has been trying to get people's attention for a long time. Even in the days of Moses God told the people through prophets how He called forth the mighty Egyptian army with all its chariots and horses and how he drew them beneath the waves and drowned them to protect His people. God told them how He had more in store.

> **Isaiah 43:18-19 (NLT)** [18] "But forget all that — it is nothing compared to what I am going to do. [19] For I am about to do something new. See, I have already begun! Do you not see it? I will make a pathway through the wilderness. I will create rivers in the dry wasteland.

I'm here to tell you now as it was told to the Israelites on their way to the promise land, seize the moment because you can't go back to the way things were before you found the Lord. You now have a brighter future than what it was in the past. God can put you back on the potter's wheel and remold you. You should commit yourself to God. Then He will open doors to new vision and new possibilities.

Conclusion

We all go through things in our lives. Even the best of lives have had to stumble along the way. You should have the wisdom to know that all you've been through has made you the person you are and it all had meaning and purpose. Sometimes the things you have to deal with has little to do with you. You may have been placed in a certain position or situation so you can help or advice someone else. As a Christian, you will sometimes face adversity just because of your status as a Christian. I know it will be hard to do but you should see some of the attacks as a good thing because those people who are doing the attacking have seen something in you (Christ) that bothers them. The good part of this is that you're living a life where these people are seeing that you're different.

> **1 Peter 4:12-14 (NLT)** ¹²Dear friends, don't be surprised at the fiery trials you are going through, as if something strange were happening to you. ¹³Instead, be very glad—for these trials make you partners with Christ in his suffering, so that you will have the wonderful joy of seeing his glory when it is revealed to all the world. ¹⁴So be happy when you are insulted for being a Christian, for then the glorious Spirit of God rests upon you.

God will help you recover from your stumble. He sometimes places you in that position so that you can see His glory. Otherwise, you would think it was your own efforts that fixed your problem and not give God the credit. Shake your problems off and get ready to be strong!

> **1 Samuel 2:4 (NLT)** 4 The bow of the mighty is now broken, and those who stumbled are now strong.

When you gain Godly wisdom, there are four revolutionary ways God will change your life.

1. Those who have stumbled are going to be strong
2. Those that were hungry, are going to be full
3. Those who were barren are about to produce
4. God will lift the poor out of the dust

Keep in mind being poor doesn't necessarily mean money. For example, you can be poor in spirit or poor in self-esteem. You have to let God be in control. You need to be wise enough to allow others to give you positive criticism. However, negative criticism is meant to not just kill you, but decrease your ability to produce from inside.

Some of the bad things that happen to us in our lives were meant to be good in the long run. If you would recall the Bible story of when Joseph was sold for money by his own brothers. They were jealous oh him and thought they'd got rid of him. What they didn't know was that God meant this to be a blessing to Joseph. The king Joseph belonged to trusted him so much he gave him land to rule. Joseph's family lived in an area that was stricken by famine. Joseph was living so well that his brothers did not recognize him when he saved them from starvation. Joseph later revealed his identity.

> **Genesis 45:5-7 (NLT)** ⁵But don't be upset, and don't be angry with yourselves for selling me to this place. It was God who sent me here ahead of you to preserve your lives. ⁶This famine that has ravaged the land for two years will last five more years, and there will be neither plowing nor harvesting. ⁷God has sent me ahead of you to keep you and your families alive and to preserve many survivors.

When Joseph saw his brothers begin to ponder what they had done to him, Joseph told them it was God who sent Joseph there, not them! You should start acting like the person God made you to be and don't try to fit in with those who are not saved. Realize that no matter where you go, God will give you favor. This is because God will keep the feet of the faithful. There will be a shifting in the body of Christ, so be faithful.

> **Ecclesiastes 9:17-18 (NLT)** Better to hear the quiet words of a wise person

than the shouts of a foolish king. Better to have wisdom than weapons of war, but one sinner can destroy much that is good.

There is no situation from which God can't bring you out. Being faithful in God will place you in a position to recover from anything in your past. You should strive to gain the Godly wisdom God wants you to have and to operate under. This will elevate you to continuously higher levels in your life!

References

Chambers, O. (2012, August 1). *My Utmost for His Highest.* (J. Reimann, Ed.)

DCoE. (2014, September 14). *Psychological Health.* Retrieved from Defense Centers of Excellence for Psychological Health and Traumatic Brain Injury: http://www.dcoe.mil/PsychologicalHealth/Psychological_Health_Information.aspx

Deistic evolution. (n.d.). Retrieved 2014, from Rational Wiki: http://rationalwiki.org/wiki/Deistic_evolution

Jakes, T. (2007). *So You Call Yourself a Man?: A Devotional for Ordinary Men with Extraordinary Potential.* Baker Books.

Piper, J. (2005). *Future Grace* (Paperback ed.). Sisters, OR: Multnomah Books.

Schopenhauer, A. (2004). *The Wisdom of Life* (Dover Ed ed.). (T. B. Saunders, Trans.) Dover: Dover Publications.

The American Optometric Association (AOA). (2014, May 15). *Visual Acuity: What is 20/20 Vision?* Retrieved from The American Optometric Association (AOA): http://www.aoa.org/patients-and-public/eye-and-vision-problems/glossary-of-eye-and-vision-conditions/visual-acuity?sso=y

Vaughn, L. (1993). *No Other Way, Establishing God's Standard For The Family.* Treasure House.

Wilson, F. B., & Armster, J. A. (2010). *The Power of Christian Friendship.* Mustang: Tate Publishing.

*Unless otherwise noted, all Bible references are from the New Living Life Translation (NLT).

Made in the USA
Columbia, SC
09 September 2021